Basic Filing For
Health Information
Management

Basic Filing for Health Information Management

Jan L. Johnson, B.S., C.M.A., M.T.
Instructor, Olympic College
Bremerton, Washington

Delmar Publishers' Online Services
To access Delmar on the World Wide Web, point your browser to:
http://www.delmar.com/delmar.html
To access through Gopher: gopher://gopher.delmar.com
(Delmar Online is part of "thomson.com", an Internet site with information on
more than 30 publishers of the International Thomson Publishing organization.)
For information on our products and services:
email: info@delmar.com
or call 800-347-7707

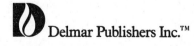

Delmar Publishers Inc.™

I(T)P™

NOTICE TO THE READER

s not warrant or guarantee any of the products described herin or perform any
analysis in connection with any of the product information contained herein. Publisher does not assume, and expressly disclaims, any obligation to obtain and include information other than that provided to it by the manufacturer.

The reader is expressly warned to consider and adopt all safety precautions that might be indicated by the activities described herein and to avoid all potential hazards. By following the instruction contained herein, the reader willingly assumes all risks in connection with such instructions.

The publisher makes no representations or warranties of an kind, including but not limited to, the warranties of fitness for particular purpose or merchantability, nor are any such representations implied with respect to the material set forth herein, and the publisher takes no responsibility with respect to such material. The publisher shall not be liable for any special, consequential or exemplary damages resulting, in whole or in part, from the reader's use of, or reliance upon, this material.

Cover design by Cronin & Prusko Visual Communications

Delmar Staff
  Executive Editor: David Gordon
  Administrative Editor: Marion Waldman
  Project Manager: Carol Micheli
  Production Coordinator: Jennifer Gaines
  Art and Design Coordinator: Timothy J. Conners

For information, address Delmar Publishers Inc.
3 Columbia Circle, Box 15-015
Albany, New York 12212

Printed in the United States of America
Published simultaneously in Canada
by Nelson Canada,
a division of The Thomson Corporation

  2 3 4 5 6 7 8 9 10 XXX 00 99 98 97 96 95

Johnson, Jan L., 1947–
  Basic filing for health information management / Jan L. Johnson.—
  1st ed
    p.   cm.
  Includes index.
  ISBN 0-8273-5457-6
  1. Medical records—Management. 2. Filing systems. I. Title
  R864.J635 1994   93-13902
  651.5'04261–dc20   CIP

Dedication:

This book is lovingly dedicated to my husband, who provided me with the encouragement to go on with my schooling, which has led to the development of this book.

Table of Contents

Preface

This manual is intended to bring together all elements involved in basic filing procedures for health information management. In teaching medical filing, I have found it difficult to find a teaching manual that contains comprehensive rules and practical application of filing procedures. The majority of the material available is either suited strictly to business application of filing or, where applicable, to processing health information, with very little in the way of practical application practice materials. This manual is intended to be of practical use in supplying the rules and giving the student hands-on practice with filing.

Fifty percent of the class hours should focus on learning alphabetic filing rules. This can most effectively be done by introducing the rules two or three at a time, grouped by relevancy. A great deal of time should be spent with transparencies, board work, and practice sheets to develop familiarity with the rules so that the students can instinctively remember the concepts before proceeding to the various types of filing systems. Reinforcement is built into instruction by spending 15 to 20 minutes of class time in practicum activities with each group before proceeding to the next group of rules. The materials are designed so that a student and/or class can proceed with assignments and select only those practice or self-study materials they feel are relevant to their learning needs.

In maintaining health information records, the primary systems utilized include the various types of color-coded systems and numeric systems. Therefore, the bulk of the practical applications in this manual will focus on using those systems. In addition, phonetic, subject, and geographic filing systems are presented briefly. The latter three systems are employed primarily to maintain health information for research and disease control. In addition, clinics and hospitals with large volumes of patients and doctors doing research studies would maintain these types of files.

Next, we will take a brief look at "maintenance" of files and use of the computer in maintaining patient database files. Once the rules and systems are well ingrained, the students can begin to work with processing the charts, which entails introducing procedures for filing materials. In this section, the students will first receive practical experience in processing the material so that it can be filed correctly; they will then file the charts in proper sequence using an appropriate filing system.

The last unit deals with filing procedures of correspondence. Here the students bring together their filing rules and procedures, and the concepts of incoming and outgoing correspondence are introduced. Inasmuch as this is a complicated concept for many of the students to grasp, it is recommended that board work and transparencies be used for drills initially, with progression to group project work and individual work. Sample correspondence is provided as practice material.

Although many offices adopt their own filing "rules," the rules presented here are in accordance with ARMA (Association of Records Managers and Administrators). These rules are periodically updated, so it is important that you keep abreast of current rules and changes to them. **With reference to filing of patient charts only**, exception is taken to the rule regarding "as written" or "the name the patient goes by," because all medical charts must be filed by the patient's legal name.

My deepest gratitude is extended to everyone who has made publication of this textbook a reality—to Marti Lewis who has given me encouragement in all my endeavors; to the many health information specialists and medical assistants who participated in the surveys; and to the reviewers who provided the important details I overlooked. My special thanks to Paul and Kari for their patience while I spent countless hours at the computer and doing research.

Introduction

It is important that much emphasis be placed on the alphabetic filing rules because all of the filing systems evolve around them. A student who has an excellent grasp of the filing rules can become proficient and effective at filing of charts and other medical records. Through the utilization of efficient procedures, fewer records are lost and the employee is freed up to attend to other tasks.

This manual is designed to provide the student with as much practical application of the filing procedures as possible in a limited amount of training time. It is my intent that the manual be used either in a classroom situation, in a clinic situation or as a self-paced handbook by individuals.

The content of the book includes a thorough presentation and review of the alphabetic filing rules, including the special applications necessary for individual medical charts. After a presentation of the alphabetic rules, the student is introduced to filing procedures, common filing systems, and correspondence-filing procedures. It is my experience in the teaching field that immediate and practical application provides students with the most long-lasting retention of what they have learned. Therefore, at the end of the alphabetic rules chapter, there are self-study exams which students can use to study for tests and reinforce their learning.

There are several appendices to be used in conjunction with classroom work and/or office situations. Appendix A contains keys to the self-study exams. Appendix B contains wet-and-stick labels to be used with the color-coding exercises. Appendix C contains materials required for the filing activities. Appendix D illustrates various methods used to organize patient charts. Appendix E contains samples of label methods that various offices/clinics use to set up chart labels for their patients.

Objectives

Upon completion of this course, the student will be able to:

- Identify common filing terms.
- Demonstrate understanding of filing systems by applying alphabetic rules.
- List elements required in numeric filing systems.
- Recognize what files need to be cross-referenced.
- Identify steps in filing procedures.
- Use correct procedures for filing incoming and outgoing correspondence.
- Explain the use of the computer for patient database files.

UNIT 1

Filing Fundamentals

Objectives

1. Explain common filing terms.
2. Distinguish types of file folder cuts.
3. State three reasons for accurately maintaining files.
4. Identify guide positions.

Vocabulary

- **Accession Record** (numeric system)—Logbook used to assign numbers to correspondence or patients.

- **"As Written"**—Refers to the name a patient might use rather than his or her legal name, e.g. Chuck rather than Charles or Mrs. Robert Downs rather than Stephanie Downs.

- **Charge Out–Follow Up**—A system of processing requests for health information to ensure return of information.

- **Coding**—Process of marking the indexing units to indicate how information is to be filed:

  Alpha filing: 3   2   1
                     Serjevo   Claire   Marie

  Subject filing: Letter from medical supply house—coded with "Medical Supplies"

- **Color Coding**—A method of filing that utilizes colors to ensure quick filing and retrieval of records. Two common methods are the *Tab Alpha Code System* and a *color-coded file folders.*

  EXAMPLE:
  Using the Tab Alpha Code System, names would be assigned colored labels as follows:

Patient Name	Color-Coded Label
Caton	orange C and brown A
Cemak	orange C and green E
Tesler	purple T and green E

  Using a *color-coded folder system*, for instance in a clinic with several doctors, each doctor's patient would be given a file folder color coded to the doctor.

Doctor	Patient Files
Dr. Smith	yellow folders
Dr. Allenstein	purple folders
Dr. Watson	red folders

- **Correspondence**—Incoming and outgoing health information in written form.

- **Cross-Reference**—A notation in a file directing the reader to a specific record that may be filed under more than one name/subject, e.g. married name vs. maiden name, or a foreign name in which the surname is not easily recognizable.

- **Guide**—A sheet or card with a captioned tab used to separate sections in a file.

- **Indexing**—Selecting the name, subject or number under which to file a record and determining the order in which the units should be considered.

- **Inspection**—Looking carefully at the item to be filed in order to identify the key name, business, subject, etc., to which the information relates.
- **Key Unit**—The first indexing unit of the filing segment.
- **Out Sheet**—A card, folder, or slip of paper inserted temporarily in the files to replace a record that has been retrieved from the files.
- **Phonetic Filing**—A method of filing that is a variation of a numeric system, utilizing letters and numbers and in which sounds are assigned numbers. A four-digit alphanumeric code is used for filing purposes.

  EXAMPLE:

Name	*Alpha-Numeric Label*
Johnson	J525
Johnsen	J525
Sorenson	S652

- **Release Mark**—A symbol, usually in the form of initials, a code, or a stamp, indicating that the material (letter, lab report, insurance form, etc.) is ready to be filed.
- **Surname**—A person's last name.
- **Tickler File**—A system designed to remind one of action to be taken on a certain date.
- **Unit**—Each part of a name (business or person) or words that will be indexed and coded for filing.

File Folders

File folders are designed for different types of labels. Extending along the top edge (the edge that will be visible when filing) are tabs which are cut in varying sizes to allow for different methods of labeling. These tabs are referred to as "cuts." Below are identified the types of "cuts" found on folders.

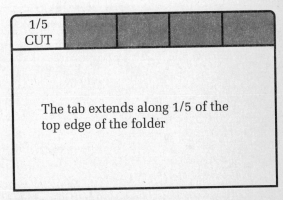

Figure 1-1 *One-fifth cut*

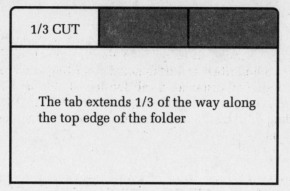

Figure 1-2 *One-third cut*

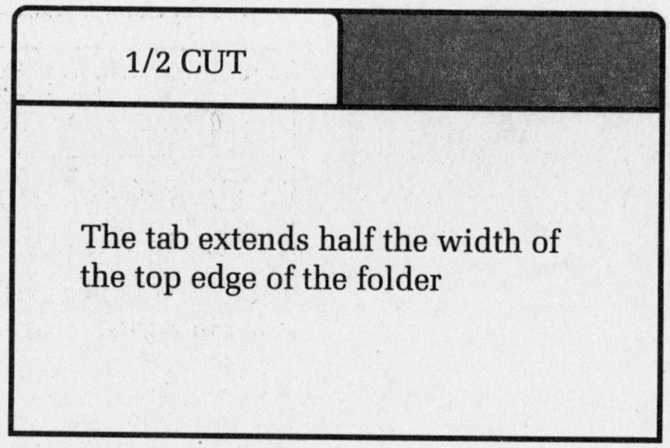

The tab extends 1/3 of the way along the top edge of the folder

1/3 CUT

1/2 CUT

The tab extends half the width of the top edge of the folder

Figure 1-3 *One-half cut*

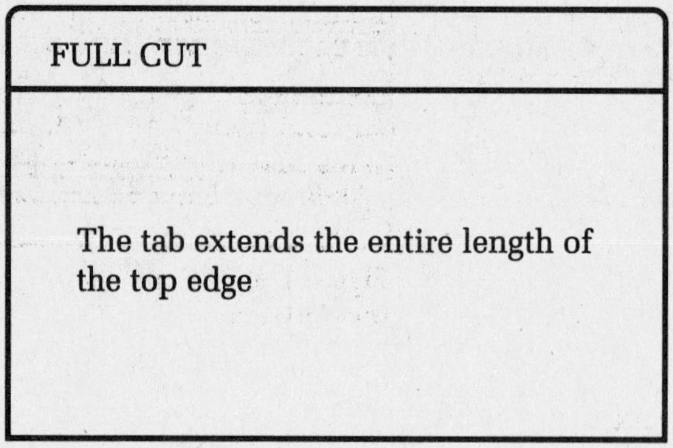

FULL CUT

The tab extends the entire length of the top edge

Figure 1-4 *Full cut*

Guides and Positions

To separate the file folders in some manner, we use what are called *guides*. The guides are somewhat larger than the file folders and are of a heavier stock. These are described and designated according to the *position* in which the tab is located. For instance, a tab located at the far left would be in the first position, the next one to the right would be in the second position, etc. If you are using third-cuts, you have three positions of guides; if using fifth-cuts, five positions.

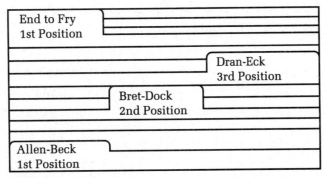

Figure 1-5 *Filing using one-third cuts*

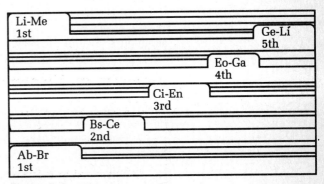

Figure 1-6 *Filing using one-fifth cuts*

Captions

Captions are utilized in the files to break the major sections (alpha, states, disease, etc.) into more manageable subunits (AA-AC, cities, communicable–airborne, etc). These are denoted as single-caption and double caption.

Single Captions contain just one letter or number:
Alpha: A, B, C, D
Numeric: 25, 50, 75, 100
Geographical: Alabama, California

Double Captions contain a double notation to denote a range of files:
Alpha: Ab-Be, Co-Dy, Ho-Le
Numeric: 1-25, 50-100, 100-500
Geographical: Alabama–California

Why's and Wherefore's of Accurate Filing

Medical files are the life and breath of a health care facility. Accurate filing of patient charts is the only method by which a facility can efficiently track information vital to the care of the patient. The potential for medical litigation dictates that every health care facility have an efficient filing system as well as personnel who can utilize and maintain that filing system of records.

First and foremost, a doctor can provide the best care for patients if all pertinent data are readily accessible. This means the personnel in charge of filing and retrieving those records must be able to file the information within the patient's chart as well as to know the filing system in order to facilitate location of the file each and every time the record is required.

Let us say that patient Althea Brownley is seen on Tuesday morning by Doctor Yesler (her general practitioner) for acute stomach pain. She is given a thorough examination by the doctor and sent for appropriate testing, to be performed that afternoon. She is then scheduled for a followup appointment on Friday with Doctor Yesler and an appointment with a gastroenterologist on Friday afternoon, if required. The tests are performed and the results are received from the outside laboratory. However, Ms. Brownley's chart has not been filed properly so the results are set aside until the chart can be located. Friday arrives and Ms. Brownley comes back to the office for her appointment, obviously worried and anxious to know the results of her tests. Doctor Yesler reviews the file, which has been routed to him, but it lacks the test results because they could not be incorporated into the records earlier in the week.

Doctor Yesler is now in the office with his patient—who is already distraught and probably not in a totally rational state of mind—and is unable to provide the test results. (The person who received the test results is not in the office at the time.) Although the test results have not been lost, they are certainly not of any value at this point to either the doctor or the patient. Meanwhile, the doctor is highly distressed with the staff as well as embarrassed because he is unable to provide the immediate care to the patient; the patient is further upset. In this case, the tests can be located readily upon the return to the office of the staff member who initially received them. Needless to say, though, the doctor was unable to provide the best possible care to his patient as a result of something as "simple" as a filing oversight.

While this may seem an uncommon scenario, it is actually all too common in large offices and clinics where records cannot be closely monitored by only one or two individuals. A student of mine once reported that one of the offices she worked in had a "filing system" that was a repository for miscellaneous reports when proper charts could not be located—some of the reports being "filed" there for months at a time.

Patient files are essential to patient care beyond the need for them in, for example, the primary care medical office. In this day and age of specialization, many patients with acute medical problems are referred to one or more specialists, who need to be able to coordinate their care. Each treating physician needs to be aware of what tests were performed and what diagnoses have been made. This not only allows physicians to provide the most efficient care but also it is absolutely essential in terms of controlling medical care costs.

Obviously beyond the problem of doctor–patient relationship are the legal issues that face every medical office and its employees today. The unfortunate conclusion in medical law is that if there is not a written record of a temperature, a visit, history and physical, lab report, and so forth, then the procedure did not happen. This means that, to be prepared in the event of medical litigation, a medical facility must be able to document any and all medical treatment performed. No matter how well a doctor has performed treatment, if a written record cannot prove how and what was done, there is no basis for a defense in a court of law.

Additionally, although we tend to think of patient files as relating solely to the patient's care or to legal issues, patient records are also essential to provide clinical data for education and research purposes. Epidemiologists and researchers depend on solid facts that they can obtain only from the records of the day-to-day care of patients. This means they require well-maintained, accurate files that show the complete details of medical procedures.

UNIT **2**

Alphabetic Filing Rules

Objectives

1. Discuss application of alphabetic filing rules.
2. Apply alphabetic rules in order to index and code individual names.
3. Apply alphabetic rules in order to index and code organizations and businesses.
4. Explain how the "as written" rule affects the labeling and filing of patient charts.

It is essential that there be some organized method of identifying and breaking down items to be filed into small, subunits. This is accomplished "through the use of what we call indexing. In this process each unit is identified according to unit 1, unit 2, unit 3, etc., with each segment of the filing label identified. This process can be applied to individual names, organizations, clinics, etc. As we proceed through the filing rules, you will see *how* we assign unit numbers to each element.

PAUL	DOUGLAS	ALLAN	SWENLAND
Unit 1			Swenland
Unit 2			Paul
Unit 3			Douglas
Unit 4			Allan

The following items to be filed would be assigned units as illustrated:

GIVEN NAME	UNITS ASSIGNED			
	1	*2*	*3*	*4*
Patrick S. Duffy	**Duffy**	Patrick	S	
Doctors Clinic	**Doctors**	Clinic		
Redstone Medical Supply	**Redstone**	Medical	Supply	
Kari Sue Lynn Jones	**Jones**	Kari	Sue	Lynn
AAA Patient Services	**AAA**	Patient	Services	
XYZ Supplies	**X**	Y	Z	Supplies

At this point do not be concerned with *how* we have arrived at units 1, 2, etc. What is important is that you recognize that each separate segment must be assigned a number.

* *

NOTE: In filing *medical charts*, the patient's *legal name* is *always* used. Rules 2, 3, and 6 below, therefore, apply to filing/labeling of materials other than patient charts—such as with miscellaneous correspondence received in the office, employment applications, inquiries, magazines, private letters, and so forth. You will always obtain a patient's legal name for their chart and index that rather than "as written.".

* *

Individual Names

Rule 1: The names of individuals are assigned indexing units respectively: last name (surname), first name, middle name and succeeding names.

GIVEN NAME	UNITS ASSIGNED			
	1	*2*	*3*	*4*
Alice Leigh Stetson	**Stetson**	Alice	Leigh	
Samuel Aaron Burtzen	**Burtzen**	Samuel	Aaron	
Carol Sue Marie Jones	**Jones**	Carol	Sue	Marie
Susan Alway Beeson	**Beeson**	Susan	Alway	
Sam Evans Nicholson	**Nicholson**	Sam	Evans	

Rule 2: If the item you are indexing uses an *initial* rather than a complete name, *index it as it is written.*

GIVEN NAME	UNITS ASSIGNED			
	1	*2*	*3*	*4*
Allison P. Cole	**Cole**	Allison	P	
S. Allan Brady	**Brady**	S	Allan	
P. T. Barnum	**Barnum**	P	T	
Everett T. J. Maxim	**Maxim**	Everett	T	J

Rule 3: If the item you are indexing uses *abbreviations or nicknames* rather than a complete name, *index it as it is written.*

GIVEN NAME	UNITS ASSIGNED			
	1	*2*	*3*	*4*
Phil T. Collins	**Collins**	Phil	T	
Sue P. Marie Thomas	**Thomas**	Sue	P	Marie
Bob Samson Fenteson	**Fenteson**	Bob	Samson	
Tess Jeane Marley	**Marley**	Tess	Jeane	

Assignment • 1

Take the list of names found in Appendix C numbered 1–20 and proceed as follows:

1. Make an index card for each of the 20 names by writing each name in the top left-hand section of a separate 3″ × 5″ card (or 3″ × 5″ slips of paper), in proper indexing order.

   EXAMPLE: 5   Allison   Jeanne   O'Kenney

                                    2   **3**

              <u>OKENNEY</u>   Allison   Jeanne

2. Underline the *key unit* and number the remaining units in the order they would be used for filing.

3. Set up a mini filing system by using the alphabetic tab guides provided in Appendix B. This can be done by using a recipe box or any other container that will hold approximately 150 cards.

4. File cards 1–20 in their proper filing order.

5. Complete the following questions after the cards have been properly filed. List the answers to the questions on a separate sheet of paper for comparison with the teacher's guide.
   a. Which card precedes #16?
   b. What is the second filing unit for card #9?
   c. What is the third filing unit for card #3?
   d. Which card is found directly behind card #5?
   e. How many cards are found in the "B" section?

If you had difficulty with the filing or indexing order of any of the names, refer back to the individual rule that relates to the indexing of the individual's name. Then compare your labeling or filing to the rules to clarify how each name was properly indexed and/or filed.

Rule 4: *Prefixes and foreign language prefixes are indexed as one unit with the unit that follows. Spacing, punctuation, and capitalization are ignored. Such prefixes include d, da, de, de la, del, des, di, du, el, fitz, l, la, las, le, les, lu, m, mac, mc, o, saint, sainte, san, santa, sao, st, te, ten, ter, van, van de, van der, and von der. (*St, sainte, saint are indexed as written.)*

GIVEN NAME	UNITS ASSIGNED			
	1	*2*	*3*	*4*
Emerson P. O'Malley	**Omalley**	Emerson	P	
Oscar De'Laurent	**Delaurent**	Oscar		
Maria R. Del Salvo	**Desalva**	Maria	R	
Victor D. St. James	**Stjames**	Victor	D	
Kelly M. Saint James	**Saintjames**	Kelly	M	
Kathy Lynn Mac Adams	**Macadams**	Kathy	Lynn	

Practice

For the following names identify the first, second, and third indexing units. *Remember to disregard spacing, punctuation and capitalization.*

EXAMPLE:
Susan B. Anthony

> **Anthony Susan B**

Name

Allisson Luanne Walsh-Blevins

Carol Jean St. Thomas

Geraldine Sue-Ellyn Cash

Parker W. Saint Thomas

Tom Allan Spencer

Gerald Daven-Havens

Proper Indexing Order

Thomas Allan Dodd

Mason Porder Westoff

Monica J. Hart

William Daniel Manta

Ivan Bortell-Romano

Martha Jane duLac

Jamie Lee Thompson

Steven Hargrade-McDonald

Rule 5: Titles are considered as separate indexing units. If the *title appears with first and last name, the title is considered to be the last indexing unit.*

GIVEN NAME	UNITS ASSIGNED			
	1	*2*	*3*	*4*
Dr. Allan B. Moore	**Moore**	Allan	B	(Dr)*
Prof. Alex P. Trebeck	**Trebeck**	Alex	P	(Prof)
Capt. Harry Calmback	**Calmbeck**	Harry	(Capt)	
Ms. Kathleen Triole	**Triole**	Kathleen	(Ms)	

****

NOTE: **Title is listed in parentheses after the last indexing unit. (We use the rule applying to names with titles, because in a health care setting it is not practical to process information with a title but no first name.)**

****

Rule 6a: Names that are *hyphenated* are *considered as one unit* (see also cross-referencing unit).

GIVEN NAME	UNITS ASSIGNED			
	1	*2*	*3*	*4*
Ms. Anna Wry-Yost	**Wryyost**	Anna	Ms	
Alisa M. Case-Bitt	**Casebitt**	Alisa	M	
Edwin Q. Mist-Fein	**Mistfein**	Edwin	Q	
Cindy-Marie Brown	**Brown**	Cindymarie		

> **Rule 6b:** When indexing the name of a *married woman*, the name is indexed *as used*. If the woman is known by her first name and her surname, these would be the indexing units. However, if the woman uses the title "Mrs.," her husband's first name, and then the surname, these would be the primary indexing units for filing purposes (see cross-referencing).

GIVEN NAME	UNITS ASSIGNED			
	1	*2*	*3*	*4*
Mrs. Sallie P. Porter	**Porter**	Sallie	P	(Mrs)
Ms. Lori T. Armor	**Armor**	Lori	T	(Ms)
Mrs. Donald R. Swan	**Swan**	Donald	R	(Mrs)
Mrs. Arnold Grensley	**Grensley**	Arnold	(Mrs)	

> **Rule 7a:** *Seniority units* are indexed as the *last indexing unit*.*

GIVEN NAME	UNITS ASSIGNED			
	1	*2*	*3*	*4*
John Thomas Moore II	**Moore**	John	Thomas	II
Dennis P. Wexler, Jr.	**Wexler**	Dennis	P	Jr

Rule 7b: *Seniority units are filed in numerical order from first to last.*

GIVEN NAME	UNITS ASSIGNED			
	1	*2*	*3*	*4*
Wm. Eric Sloan III before	**Sloan**	Wm	Eric	III
Wm. Eric Sloan IV	**Sloan**	Wm	Eric	IV
Jesse Ray William, Jr. before	**William**	Jesse	Ray	Jr
Jesse Ray William, Sr.	**William**	Jesse	Ray	Sr

****

***NOTE:* In case of identical names without seniority designations, health care facilities use a variety of methods for the indexing order including: date of birth, social security number, or addresses (see Rule 14).**

****

Rule 7c: These numeric units are broken down such that *numeric seniority terms are filed before alphabetic terms.*

GIVEN NAME	UNITS ASSIGNED			
	1	*2*	*3*	*4*
Kent O. Van Nuys, II before	**Vannuys**	Kent	O	II
Kent O. Van Nuys, Jr. before	**Vannuys**	Kent	O	Jr
Kent O. Van Nuys, Sr.	**Vannuys**	Kent	O	Sr

Practice

Utilizing the alphabetic filing rules, identify how the following names would be correctly labeled for *patient chart files*; write on the right-hand side of the page the proper indexing order to be used for the patient's chart label. Indicate the proper alphabetic filing order by marking the labels from 1-10.

Part A:

Patient Chart Files

EXAMPLE: Albert A. (Legal Name: Astin) Anderson

Label: | **ANDERSON** Albert Astin #1 |

Order	**Label**
Michael V. (Victor) Swanson	
Sue Elaine Michaels	
Capt. Murray T. Leskowsky	
Michelle-Suzanne O'Reilly	
Mrs. Robert Burdett (Claire)	
Hollister McKenzie, III	
Eddie Swiback-Hudson	
Mrs. Suzanne Murray (Paul)	
Edward Anthony MacCall	
Hollister McKenzie, Jr.	
Carmella E. deLasandro	

Part B:

General Filing using ARMA rules

Complete labels for those patients whose labels would be typed differently than for a patient file.

```
┌─────────────────┐  ┌─────────────────┐  ┌─────────────────┐
│                 │  │                 │  │                 │
└─────────────────┘  └─────────────────┘  └─────────────────┘

┌─────────────────┐  ┌─────────────────┐  ┌─────────────────┐
│                 │  │                 │  │                 │
└─────────────────┘  └─────────────────┘  └─────────────────┘

┌─────────────────┐  ┌─────────────────┐  ┌─────────────────┐
│                 │  │                 │  │                 │
└─────────────────┘  └─────────────────┘  └─────────────────┘
```

Assignment • 2

Take the list of names found in Appendix C numbered 21-40 and proceed as follows:

1. Make an index card for each of the names by writing each name in the top left-hand section of a separate 3″ × 5″ card (or 3″ × 5″ slips of paper), in proper indexing order.

2. Place all of the labeled cards in the proper indexing order along with cards #1–20.

3. Answer the following questions regarding the filed cards. List the answers to the questions on a separate sheet of paper for comparison with the teacher's guide.
   a. For card #37 what is the third indexing unit?
   b. How many indexing units are there for card #25?
   c. Which card is located directly in front of card #26?
   d. Which cards would be filed behind the letter "H" guide?
   e. List the card found directly in front of card #23.
   f. Which card would be filed first, #40 or #30?
   g. Which cards (list in order) are found in the files between #25 and #40?
   h. How many files are located in the letter "M" section?
   i. Which would be filed first, card #39 or #23?
   j. How many indexing units are there for card #37?

If you wish to review before taking test #1, you may work on the three self-study exams at the end of the chapter. These relate to the first seven alphabetic filing rules. The answers are found in Appendix A.

Businesses and Organizations

When indexing businesses and organizations, the rules you have learned under *individual names* will be used when individual names appear as part of the filing units (rules 1–7). In addition there are several rules which we will introduce not relevant to individuals.

Rule 8: The *order* for indexing businesses/organizations is *as written.**

| GIVEN NAME | UNITS ASSIGNED | | | |
	1	2	3	4
Brown's Medical Supply	**Browns**	Medical	Supply	
Acme Surgical Tools	**Acme**	Surgical	Tools	
VA Memorial Hospital	**VA**	Memorial	Hospital	
Wildwood Convalescent	**Wildwood**	Convalescent		
X-Ray Associates	**Xray**	Associates		
A B C Florists	**A**	B	C	Florists

****

NOTE: **Use company letterhead as a guide.**

****

Rule 9: When "the" is the first unit of a business/organization, it is *indexed as the last unit.*

1. The A-1 Medical Records Company
   Indexed as:
   A1   Medical   Records   Company   The
2. The Records Manager
   Indexed as:
   Records   Manager   The
3. Aids for the Disabled
   Indexed as:
   Aids   For   The   Disabled

The point of the first indexing unit is that it will quickly narrow the search for the appropriate file. Thus, other common first units such as "a" and "an" would also be last as they would not be of significance in locating the appropriate file.

Rule 10a: *Symbols* are indexed as units and *spelled out as words.* Such symbols include &, ¢, $, #, and %.

GIVEN NAME	ASSIGNED DESIGNATION
&	AND
¢	CENT or CENTS
&	DOLLAR or DOLLARS
#	NUMBER or POUNDS
%	PERCENT

Rule 10b: In indexing the "$" sign *before a number, the first unit is the number.*

GIVEN NAME	ASSIGNED ORDER		
$50 Resort	50DOLLAR	Resort	
$2 Bargain Center	2DOLLAR	Bargain	Center

Rule 11: When *punctuation marks* are included as part of the indexing units, they are *disregarded.* Punctuation marks include: . " ' : ; - ! ? ( ).

GIVEN NAME	ASSIGNED ORDER		
Radburn's Janitorial	**Radburns**	Janitorial	
Lindy's Pharmaceutical	**Lindys**	Pharmaceutical	
Swit-James Memorial	**Switjames**	Memorial	
Do It! Lab Testers	**Doit**	Lab	Testers
Need Help? Counseling Service	**Need**	Help	Counseling Service

Assignment • 3

Take the list of names found in Appendix C numbered 41-60 and proceed as follows:

1. Make an index card for each of the names by writing each name in the top left-hand section of a separate 3″ × 5″ card (or 3″ × 5″ slips of paper), in proper indexing order.

2. Place all of the labeled cards in the proper indexing order along with cards #1–40.

3. Answer the following questions regarding the filed cards. List the answers to the questions on a separate sheet of paper for comparison with the teacher's guide.
   a. How many indexing units are there for card #52?
   b. What is the card found directly behind card #59?
   c. What is the proper order for the cards found under the letter "S"?
   d. Which cards are found between card #46 and #17?
   e. What is the third indexing unit for card #59?
   f. Which card is found directly behind card #18 in the files?
   g. Which cards are found under the letter "B"?
   h. What is the proper order of the files in the letter "B"?
   i. What card is found directly in front of card #47?
   j. What are the three cards that immediately follow card #42?

> Rule 12a: When indexing *numbers*, the numbers are indexed *as written*.

GIVEN NAME	ASSIGNED ORDER			
12* Street Med Supply	**12**	Street	Med	Supply
XII* Star Stationers	**XII**	Star	Stationers	
Twenty-third Ave Clinic	**Twentythird**	Ave	Clinic	

****

NOTE: **Arabic numerals are filed before Roman numerals.**

****

> Rule 12b: When indexing *figures*, the numbers are *written as figures and considered as one unit. Note*: d, nd, rd, st, and th are ignored when indexing.

GIVEN NAME	ASSIGNED ORDER		
43rd Street Pharmacy	**43**	Street	Pharmacy
22nd Avenue Clinic	**22**	Avenue	Clinic

Rule 12c: When indexing *numbers*, if the number is written as a single word it is *indexed as a single unit.*

GIVEN NAME	ASSIGNED ORDER		
Wiskah 4 Suppliers	**Wiskah**	4	Suppliers

Rule 12d: When indexing *numbers*, if the number is *written with a word*, it is *indexed as one unit with the word and filed in ascending order before alphabetic names.*

GIVEN NAME	ASSIGNED ORDER		
4Seasons Florist	**4seasons**	Florist	
The 20-Day Program	**20day**	Program	The

Rule 12e: When indexing *hyphenated numbers*, they are indexed *only by the number before the hyphen.*

GIVEN NAME	ASSIGNED ORDER		
7–12 Answering Service	**7**	Answering	Service
8–5 Medical Secretaries	**8**	Medical	Secretaries

Rule 12f: When indexing *alpha characters and numeric characters,* the *numeric characters* are always filed *before alpha characters.*

GIVEN NAME	ASSIGNED ORDER		
42nd Street Linen before	**42**	Street	Linen
63rd Avenue Hospital before	**63**	Avenue	Hospital
Fifteenth Street Supplies	**Fifteenth**	Street	Supplies

> **Rule 13:** When indexing words which can be *compound or two single words*, the *"as written"* rule applies. (Consider whether it is appropriate to cross-reference hyphenated words.)

GIVEN NAME	ASSIGNED ORDER		
Southeast Hospital	**Southeast**	Hospital	
South East Hospital	**South**	East	Hospital
West-End Supplies	**Westend**	Supplies	
West End Labs	**West**	End	Labs

> **Rule 14:** When *names* of business/clinics, etc. are *identical*, the *address may be used for ordering of the files.** The address is indexed by:
>
> *CITY → STATE → STREET NAME → ADDRESS #*

1. Acme Drug Supply, 839 Kentucky Boulevard, Crawford, Missouri
2. Acme Drug Supply, 1539 Wildflower Avenue, Fairbanks, Alaska
3. Acme Drug Supply, 742 Terminal Street West, Fairbanks, Arizona
4. Acme Drug Supply, 731 Terminal Street East, New York, New York
5. Acme Drug Supply, 683 Wildflower Avenue, Fairbanks, Alaska

These would be filed as:

- Using city first: C, F, F, N, F
- F for 2, 3 and 5 so proceed to state: Alaska, Arizona

- #5 and 3 have same city and state so proceed to street name: Wildflower
- With identical street names proceed to address: 683, 1539
  1 Crawford
  5 Fairbanks → Alaska → Wildflower → 683
  2 Fairbanks → Alaska → Wildflower → 1539
  3 Fairbanks → Arizona
  4 New York

****

NOTE: **Some facilities choose to file identical names by birth date or social security number rather than address as this remains constant.**

****

Assignment • 4

Take the list of names found in Appendix C numbered 61–80 and proceed as follows:

1. Make an index card for each of the names by writing each name in the top left-hand section of a separate 3″ × 5″ card (or 3″ × 5″ slips of paper), in proper indexing order.

2. Place all of the labeled cards in the proper indexing order along with cards #1–60.

3. Answer the following questions regarding the filed cards. List the answers to the questions on a separate sheet of paper for comparison with the teacher's guide.
   a. Under what division is card #73 found?
   b. Which cards would be found under the "V" files?
   c. What is the correct order of cards #66, 75, & 40?
   d. Which three cards would be found just preceding #11?
   e. Under what division would you find card #44?
   f. Which of the following cards would be located under the same letter division—21, 28, 51, 79?
   g. List the proper filing order of cards #21, 4, and 15.
   h. Name the first unit which gives the correct filing order for cards #74 and 79.
   i. Which card is found first in alphabetic order—#61 or #67?
   j. If you were to add another card for "Access To You" to the files, would it be located in front or in back of card #76?

_____

If you wish to review before taking test #2, you may work on the self-study exam. The answers are found in Appendix A.

Self-Study: Patient Chart Filing

Part A:

Prepare proper alpha labels for the following patient charts.

Remember: In preparing the charts, you **must use the legal name**. (LN denotes legal name.)

EXAMPLE:
Chuck (LN Charles) B. (LN) Knox

Label:

KNOX	Charles	B

GIVEN NAME	LABEL
1. Diane V. (LN) Brown	
2. Edgar A. (LN Allen) St. Leason	
3. Cullen Thomas di Salvo	
4. Mandy-Louise T. (LN Teresa) Dawson	
5. Larry (LN Lawrence) P (LN) Brocerick-O'Reilly	
6. Ned Parker McAdams	
7. Chuck (LN) Al (LN Albert) Trevontaine	
8. Jean-Marie Saint Vincent	
9. Dr. Herbert Brown	
10. Ann-Marie Sue (LN Suzanne) Tochetti	

Part B:

List the names from Part A in proper alphabetic filing order.

1.
2.
3.
4.
5.
6.
7.
8.
9.
10.

Self-Study: Alpha Filing, Rules 1—3

Part A:

List the following names in proper indexing order:

NAME	PROPER INDEXING ORDER
Gene Custer	
R. Allan Quigley	
Susan Marie Jones	
Stephen P. Pfeiffer	
A. S. Stevens	
Brady Allan Jones	
Thomas Edward Brady	
George B. Shaw	
Robert Chuck Adams	
Debra Louise Lindquist	

Part B:

Alphabetize the names in Part A in proper filing order.

1.
2.

3.

4.

5.

6.

7.

8.

9.

10.

Self-Study: Alpha Filing, Rules 4—5

Part A:

Identify the proper indexing units and order for the following names.

NAME   PROPER INDEXING ORDER

Edwina Suzanne Natrene

Susan P. von Adams

Marie Susan del Salva

Kellie Lucille O'Reilly

Professor Simon Kalmbeck

Lynn V. Utrect, M.D.

Reverend Alvin de Laurent

Edward Smith-Nelson

Susan-Leigh Davis

Robert Vincent MacCarty

Part B:

Arrange the names from Part A in alphabetical order.

1.

2.

3.

4.

5.

6.

7.

8.

9.

10.

Self-Study: Alpha Filing, Rules 6—7

Part A:

Arrange the following names in correct alphabetic order for filing.

NAME	PROPER INDEXING ORDER
Theodore Vincent Moore, III	
Vincent T. Las Casos, Jr.	
Mrs. Shelly E. Truckson	
Franklin D. Wolchecki, II	
Vincent T. Las Casos, Sr.	
Theodore Moore Vincent, Jr.	
Franklin D. Wolchecki, IV	
Mrs. Herbert Grunlund (Sallie)	
Vincent L. Las Casos, III	
Franklin D. Wollecki, Sr.	

Part B:

Alphabetize the names in Part A in proper filing order.

1.

2.

3.

4.

5.

6.

7.

8.

9.

10.

Self-Study: Alpha Filing, Business/Organizations

Part A:

Identify the following listings as they should be indexed. *Remember to use correct indexing characters only.*

NAME   **PROPER INDEXING ORDER**

Economy Billing Services

Alpha & Omega Medical Supplies

The Friendly Taxi Service

23rd Street Hospital

Bradley's Home Health Aides

First Street Clinic

Speedy Transcription 4-U

The Quick-Fix Consultants

Twenty-Second Answering Service

Allenmoore Medical Center,
   339 6th Avenue, Topeka Kansas

Allenmoore Medical Center,
   822 8th Avenue, Apple, Wisconsin

Allenmoore Medical Center,
   133 5th Avenue West, Topeka, Kansas

Mc-Adams Linen Supply

$20 Janitorial Service

WA Medical Supplies

Part B:

Alphabetize the names in Part A in proper filing order.

1.

2.

3.

4.

5.

6.

7.

8.

9.

10.

3

Cross-Referencing

Objectives

1. Explain why cross-referencing is important.
2. Identify three types of charts that are commonly cross-referenced.
3. Prepare cross-reference card files.

```
                        Alex M. Turnbill
                        345 Turnbill Road
                        Houston, TX 77035


September 15, 1992



Allen Steinmeist, M.D.
3310 Hollenhurst Way
San Antonio, TX 77024

Dear Dr. Steinmeist:

RE:   Kit Blackenwald

I am writing to update you on disability patient Kit Blackenwald.

As you know, the patient presented with a right L5 radiculopathy
with CT/myelogram and X-rays showing an L4-5 radiculopathy with
CT/myelogram and X-rays showing an L4-5 disc herniation.  I have
followed this man for two years.  In that period of time he has had
exacerbations.  Fortunately with conservative therapy, specifically
epidural steroids, the patient has been able to overcome his pain.

I would welcome your professional input on further management of
this patient.

Sincerely,


Alex M. Turnbill, M.D.

AMT/cd
```

Figure 3-1 *Sample Letter*

It is imperative that you be able to locate a file quickly and accurately. Therefore, if there is any doubt as to where a particular file would be located, cross-reference it. For instance, Sally Brown comes into the office, and you make a file on her. Four months following Ms. Brown's visit you receive a piece of correspondence on Mrs. Bertram Brown, no first name referenced. There is no file on a Mrs. Bertram Brown, but the letter makes clear reference to her visit in your office on May 22. No one has a clear recollection of the patient. How can you locate Mrs. Brown's files more efficiently than looking through the 120 charts you have under the name of Brown? Obviously, the most efficient method would have been to cross-reference Sally Brown when she came in for the initial visit.

This situation would also apply in instances where it is unclear what the indexing order of the patient's name should be (Yang Sing Teah), or if there are multiple names in correspondence from one of the partners in a medical consulting firm (letter from Mr. Ranscomb of Olsen, Piper & Ranscomb Associates), addressed to one of several doctors in a clinic. Other situations where cross-referencing is indicated include hyphenated names and situations in which a spouse or dependent has a different last name than the responsible party or head of the household.

The letter in Figure 3-1 is an example of correspondence received in a doctor's office. When the staff member went to file the chart, there was no record of the "Kit" mentioned in the letter. Unless someone was familiar with the patient (or had generated a cross-reference previously), it would be difficult to locate the file that actually belonged to "Reginald Blackenwald."

Cross-referencing not only saves time searching for files but also makes the filing system more efficient in that all items that might be interrelated are located within one particular file or chart. Many offices do not feel it necessary to cross-reference, but the small amount of time spent maintaining a simple cross-reference card or blank file can be time well spent when you are unable to locate a much-needed medical record.

The proper procedure for cross-referencing is as illustrated below. Several examples are offered in which cross-referencing might be used.

Procedure

▶ 1. Identify what the primary filing label should be.
▶ 2. Make a proper file to be used as the primary location for all medical records.
▶ 3. Identify one or more alternative ways the file might be located.
▶ 4. For the alternative filings, make a cross-reference sheet/card/dummy chart that lists the primary reference and refers back to the location of the primary file:

Example:
> *Blackenwald*, Kit
>
> SEE *Blackenwald, Reginald P.*

The *SEE* reference will identify where the primary file is located.

Let us take a look then at examples of various types of cross-reference files that might be used in an office.

Married Women

The primary file would be the patient's legal name with the cross-reference being listed under her husband's name.

Primary File:

> ***Brown***, Sally F. Mrs.
>
> (Bertram O'Malley)

X-Ref File:

> ***O'Malley***, Mrs. Bertram
>
> SEE ***Sally F. Brown***

Foreign Names

The primary file would be located under the patient's legal name. It is important, therefore, that you identify the first name, middle name, and surname when the patient comes for the first visit. Unless people are familiar with a particular group of names, the first, middle, and last names are often confused for each other. Again, your experience will teach you which cross-references should be set up.

Primary File:

> ***Sing***, Yange Teah

X-Ref File:

> ***Yange***, Sing Teah
>
> SEE ***Sing***, Yange Teah

X-Ref File:

> ***Teah***, Yange Sing
>
> SEE ***Sing***, Yange Teah

Hyphenated Names

With the proliferation of hyphenated names, it is not uncommon for materials to be listed under different combinations of the hyphenated name. For instance, a married woman may have records under her maiden name, her husband's surname, and her hyphenated name. Therefore, you may want to make two cross-references.

Primary File:

> *Money-Jordan*, Allison Marie

X-Ref File:

> *Money*, Allison Marie
>
> SEE *Money-Jordan*, Allison Marie

X-Ref File:

> *Jordan*, Allison Marie
>
> SEE *Money-Jordan*, Allison Marie

Multiple Listings

A great deal of correspondence is received from businesses and associations that have multiple listings of names. At times you may receive correspondence from only one of the involved parties. Rather than keeping a separate file for each, you can keep a primary file as listed on the letter and then cross-reference files for the individual names.

Primary File:

> *Olsen, Piper and Dillard Associates*

X-Ref File:

> PIPER, Richard C., M.D.
>
> SEE *Olsen, Piper and Dillard Associates*

X-Ref File:

> DILLARD, Thomas E., M.D.
>
> SEE **Olsen, Piper and Dillard Associates**

Assignment • 5

Take the list of names found in Appendix C numbered 81–90 and proceed as follows:

1. Make an index card for each of the names by writing each name in the top left-hand section of a separate 3″ × 5″ card (or 3″ × 5″ slips of paper), in proper indexing order.

2. Make cross-reference cards according to the guidelines discussed in this unit.

3. Place all of the labeled cards in the proper indexing order along with cards #1–80.

4. Answer the following questions regarding the filed cards. List the answers to the questions on a separate sheet of paper for comparison with the teacher's guide.
   a. What card would be located behind cross-reference card for #90?
   b. What card(s) would be located in front of the cross-reference card(s) for #86?
   c. What would be the second indexing unit for card #85 if you were preparing a patient chart?
   d. What is the second indexing unit for card #85 if you are using the ARMA rules for general filing?
   e. Under what alphabetic guide will you find card #88?
   f. What card numbers are found under the "D" alpha guide?
   g. How would you cross-reference card #47?
   h. Would you need to cross-reference card #24?

UNIT 4

Filing Procedures

Objectives

1. Identify steps required to file materials in files/charts.
2. Demonstrate indexing and coding of materials.
3. Explain the purpose of recording the whereabouts of health information when it is checked out.
4. List information required on charge out sheets.
5. Explain the term "release mark" and how it is used.
6. Illustrate two instances when a tickler file is used.

Procedural Steps

Several basic procedures are required to process the data sheets, laboratory requests, and so on from the time they are generated to the time the chart or file is returned to the medical records section. Learning to carry out this process efficiently by following some basic steps can save a considerable amount of time.

1. Inspection—*Carefully* look at the report to identify the patient, subject, file, etc. to whom the information belongs.

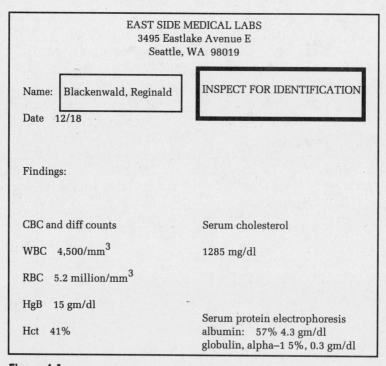

EAST SIDE MEDICAL LABS
3495 Eastlake Avenue E
Seattle, WA 98019

Name: Blackenwald, Reginald

INSPECT FOR IDENTIFICATION

Date 12/18

Findings:

CBC and diff counts

WBC 4,500/mm^3

RBC 5.2 million/mm^3

HgB 15 gm/dl

Hct 41%

Serum cholesterol

1285 mg/dl

Serum protein electrophoresis
albumin: 57% 4.3 gm/dl
globulin, alpha–1 5%, 0.3 gm/dl

Figure 4-1

2. Indexing—Use the indexing process to determine how the chart would be located, properly identifying indexing units and their order.

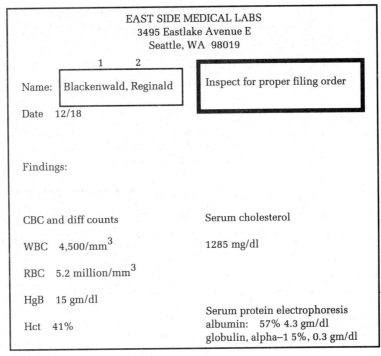

Figure 4-2

3. Coding—If using a system other than an alphabetic system, determine the proper coding (numbers, Tab-Alpha, etc.) for the chart so it can be retrieved. Otherwise, identify the indexed units by underlining, highlighting, etc. This makes refiling more effective and ensures that the item will always be filed in the same place (i.e. patient, subject, state). If a cross-reference is required, identify the cross reference by double underlining and placing an "X" nearby.

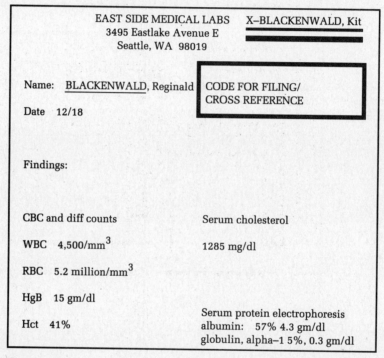

Figure 4-3

4. Sorting—If there are a number of reports or documents to be filed, sort them into units according to the captions on the charts. This will eliminate time wasted in working back and forth through the alphabet, numbers, and so forth, and will serve as a check in ensuring that the information is matched correctly with the chart.

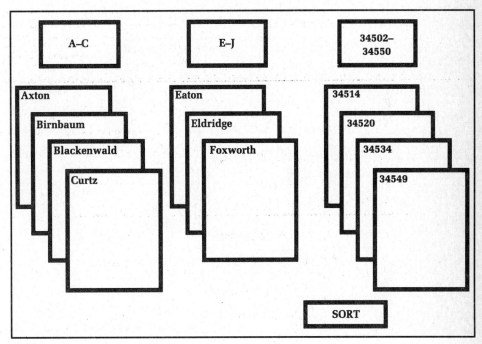

Figure 4-4

5. Filing—The papers are placed in the proper charts and the charts returned to their proper place in the medical records section. Be alert to the labels and refile any charts that have been misfiled. Be sure to verify the "release mark," indicating that all action has been completed, for example, follow-up phone call to patient, enclosure if mailing out records, etc.

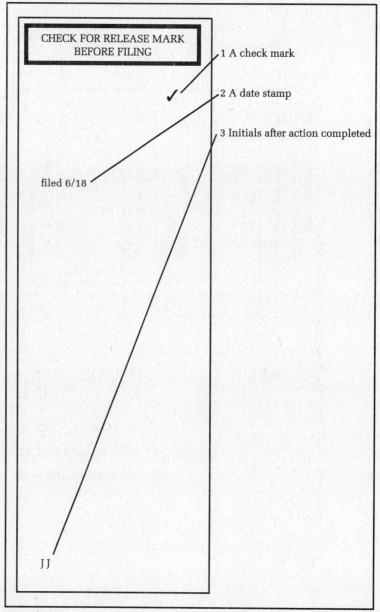

Figure 4-5

Charging Out Files

When charts are removed from the medical records department, an *Out Guide* needs to be kept in place of the patient's chart. Many offices have developed dummy charts or cardboard files labeled "Out Sheets." Most Out Guides are identified by an "Out" label or metal holder but they could be assigned a particular color; they key is that they stand out as obviously different from the primary folders. On the Out Guide there should be, at a minimum, a record of *when* the chart was *removed* and *where* the chart can be *located*.

Some offices list the expected date of return, the actual date the chart was returned, and a signature of the personnel checking out the record. There may also be a provision through a Sign-Out Sheet for certain sections of the record to be borrowed, such as a lab report or specialty examination. Below are illustrated two different types of Out Guides and a Sign-Out Sheet for this purpose.

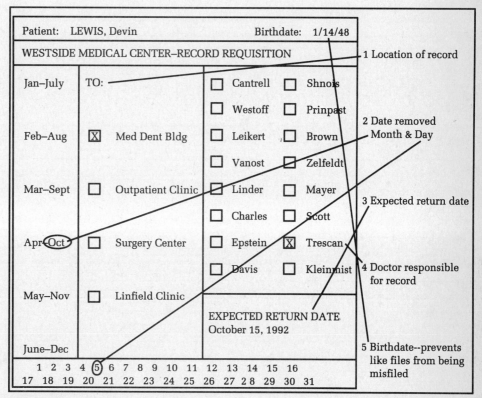

Figure 4-6 *Out Guide*

Patient: [1] Harold B. Prentiss	Date Out: [2] July 12, 1990
Birthdate: [3] 08/25/28	Date of Return: [4] August 3, 1990
Destination: [5] Dr. Rassucasseo—Seabeck Clinic	
Signature of borrower: [6]	

1 Patient of record.

2 Date borrowed.

3 Patient's birthdate--insures correct record
   is borrowed AND returned.

4 Expected date and record will be returned.

5 Knowing the location helps in locating the files if missing.

6 Signature assures someone is responsible for the record.

Figure 4-7 *Out Guide*

SIGN OUT SHEET				
Record #	Date Out	Date In	Destination	Data Borrowed
893902	4/17		Krueger	lab tests, 4/08
98832	4/17	4/17	Anderson	X-ray, 3/15/88
3771830	4/18	4/18	Show	CT scan, head
Mitzner 8/17/90	4/20		Carley	X-ray, leg
Alfonse 11/24/75	4/22	4/22	Cody	Skull X-ray
30982	4/23		Berlitz	MRI scan
Castle 3/02/48	4/29		Detweller	Blood gas study 3/18/90

The sign out sheet is retained in the medical records department. It should be accurately tracked to assure return of record data in a timely fashion.

*Note that one file checked out on 4/17 has still not been returned. Records personnel want to check on the data for an expected return date.

Figure 4-8 *Sign-Out Sheet*

Some clinics prefer to have *temporary folders* in addition to an out guide. Having a folder available makes it possible to store papers and data on a temporary basis in their correct location. These can then be filed permanently when the primary folder is returned. If these folders are of a different color or have a different type of tab/label, they can be spotted easily—which enables the staff to track the temporary files and ensure that they do not become permanent folders.

Searching for Misplaced Files

Everyone has, on occasion, wasted valuable time trying to locate a misplaced file or information. There are many reasons for misfiling, and when this situation occurs, you need to establish a procedure by which you can conduct a search for the missing information. Through a systematic search of the files, the missing data can be located a majority of the time. Be aware of the specific items you find yourself having to locate on a repeated basis. Make a note of what item(s) was misfiled and where it was located so that you can facilitate the search for similar items in the future.

To locate missing pieces of information:

- If you have the correct file but cannot find a specific item that should be located there, check all of the items within the file.
- Check other files with similar labels against the possibility that the item you seek for patient John Swanson might be filed under John E. Swanson or John Swansen.

To locate missing files:

- Look at the folders in the vicinity of (before and after) the proper location of the misplaced file.
- Look at folders with similar labels, that is, for Johnson—Johnsen, Jonson, Johanson.
- Check the doctor's desk or a desk tray where the missing file might have been left.
- If using a color-coding system, scan for folders with the same color-coding as the misplaced file.
- If using a numeric system, look for possible combinations of the numbers used in the misplaced file.

Misplaced files can be very frustrating and time consuming to locate. Your best strategy is a visual check and verification of files for proper filing order whenever you return or retrieve a file folder. In addition, when you retrieve a file folder, perhaps to answer a question on the phone, have the file folder either immediately before or after the retrieved file stick out slightly so that you can easily replace the borrowed file folder in its proper place. Most importantly, when you finish with a record, refile it immediately so it does not become lost "somewhere" in the office: A misfiled record is much easier to locate than a misplaced record.

Tickler Files

It is essential in a medical office that the office staff follow up on patients and correspondence. Sticky notes are a popular method, as is writing on the calendar, but a well-organized, efficient office will maintain what is known as a *tickler file*—in other words, a method that will remind you in the midst of your many duties to take some action on a particular date. Whether your office employs a computer with a calendar "tickler file" or whether you have a file card box, the method is still universal.

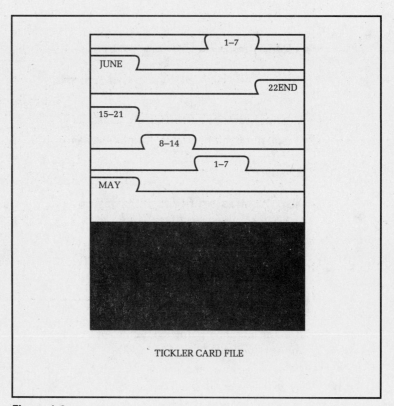

TICKLER CARD FILE

Figure 4-9

The tickler card should contain the following information:

- If the action to be taken deals with a patient or on behalf of the patient—scheduling a hospital admit or a reminder of a checkup visit—be sure to file the tickler card as soon as possible lest this task be forgotten.
- When you are filing records, be sure to look for the words "on _____ date we will," "pending action," "followup," etc., indicating that you will need to take some course of action.

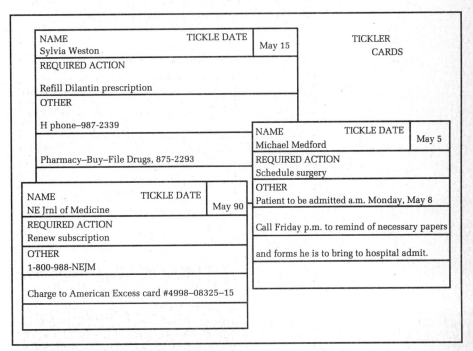

Figure 4-10

Assignment • 6

Take the items found in Appendix C for **Alpha Filing Procedures**.

Part A:

Follow steps as outlined in the procedural steps. (See pages 75–81.) Be sure to cross-reference and establish a ticker card if required.

EXAMPLE: Item—You have a copy of hospital surgery report on patient Twila B. Martinez

    1) Inspect: Information is for **patient chart**

    2) Index: *Martinez*, Twila B
                        2   3

    3) Coding: None necessary as it does not need a cross reference or tickler file

    4) Release mark: Initial or date stamp the item

    5) Place in alphabetic order behind Martinez, Joseph item to be filed alphabetically

Turn in the items, which have been filed alphabetically, along with answers to the following questions.

Part B:

1. Which items required cross-referencing?
2. Which items required a tickler card?
3. If you were unable to locate items #5 and #8, for each, list two places you could search for possible misfiling.

UNIT 5

Color-Coded
Filing Systems

Objectives

1. Explain the three major color-coding labeling systems.
2. Prepare color-coded labels using the major color-coding filing systems.
3. Provide three examples of miscellaneous color-coded filing systems.
4. Identify the major purposes for using color-coded systems.

A number of systems have been devised to assist in maintaining accurately alphabetized files. By "color coding" either the files themselves or the labels on the files, a quick glance makes it easy to locate the one that has been misfiled. We will look at the following systems utilizing color coding:

- Alpha-Z by The Smead Manufacturing Company
- Alpha-Code by Tab Products, Inc.
- Variadex by Kardex Systems, Inc.
- Variations of Color-Coding Methods

Obviously there is much diversity in these systems and there are others that have been devised. By working with these systems you will understand the principles behind color coding and you will be able to apply these principles to variations that you might encounter in an office setting.

The purpose of color coding is primarily to make retrieval of files more efficient and to make maintenance of the files more practical. Many times files are put back in haste, which leads to misfiling. Through frequent visual inspection during slack periods, you can maintain the files properly and lessen both the need for lengthy refiling sessions and your inability to locate a file.

For illustrative purposes, let us assume that David A. Ackerly is the patient for whom we are making a file. Therefore with each color-coding method, a file label for this patient will be drawn up to give you an idea of the process involved.

Alpha Code System

This method is also commonly referred to as the Tab Alpha System. The system is designed primarily for an open-shelf type arrangement although it could be utilized with a drawer set up.

Each alphabetic letter is assigned a different color. Each folder has a color-coded label. Full-cut folders are used:

- Two colored labels are used for the first two letters of the key indexing unit. (Ackerly: AK)
- A third white label contains all of the indexing units. (David A. Ackerly)
- In addition, some offices utilize a color-coded label placed on the top of the white strip to indicate the last year the patient was seen—an efficient method for easily purging files when storing outdated ones.

This particular color-coding system has several advantages. The most obvious is that misfiled charts are easily spotted and can be correctly refiled quickly and easily. The color tabs fold over the edge of the chart; therefore the labels can be seen from either the right or the left side. In addition, there are no secondary guides, simply A through Z primary guides.

Procedure

▶ 1. Type the indexing units on the white label from first to last indexing units (i.e. last name, first name, middle initial).

▶ 2. Determine the first two letters of the first indexing unit and obtain the appropriate labels.

▶ 3. Attach the coded labels to the bottom of the file tab by aligning the labels and folding over.

▶ 4. Affix the typed indexing label immediately above the coded letters.

▶ 5. Attach any additional labels (i.e. allergies, last year seen, industrial claim, etc.) to the chart according to the office procedure.

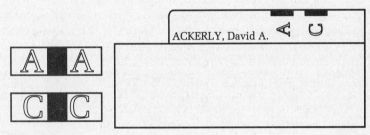

Figure 5-1

Tab-Alpha Exercise

Neatly print the label below for each file folder as it would be typed and labeled. Also indicate which colors would be visible on the label:

Alpha-Tab Coding:
A, red; B, yellow; M, blue; O, pink; E, green; S, violet; D, brown; P, purple; and F, black.

David P. Pomeroy

The Four Seasons Hotel

Allan T. Barber

Josephine Q. Mesner

Sarah De Salle

Alpha-Z System

This particular system is designed for use with either open files or drawer files. The alphabetic letters are utilized as the primary guides. Breakdowns of alphabetic combinations, as determined by the needs of a particular office, are added.

Folders have tabs with score marks for three labels:

- The first label contains the typed name, a color block, and the letter of the alphabet for the first letter of the first indexing unit.

- The second and third labels are color coded to correspond to the second and third letters of the first unit. Divisions of the alphabet are visible on extended label holders, which are attached in the top or left-hand position of guides. Out Guides are utilized in the bottom or right-hand position.

A combination of 13 colors is utilized in this system, with white letters on a colored background for the first half of the alphabet and colored letters on a white background for the second half of the alphabet.

The 13 colors utilized are as follows:

(A-M—White letter, color background)
(N-Z—Color letter, white background)

A, N	Red
B, O	Dark blue
C, P	Dark green
D, Q	Light blue
E, R	Purple
F, S	Orange
G, T	Gray
H, U	Dark brown
I, V	Pink
J, W	Yellow
K, X	Light brown
L, Y	Lavender
M, Z	Light green

EXAMPLE:

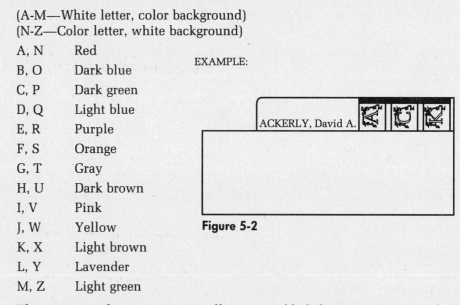

Figure 5-2

This system makes it easy to visually spot misfiled charts. However, it takes some training to familiarize the filer with the color sequences.

A possible problem is that some labels that utilize color shadings may be difficult to differentiate, for example, light, medium, and darker blue.

Procedure

▶ 1. Obtain appropriate color-coded label for the first letter of the first indexing unit:
*A*ckerly—White A on red background.

▶ 2. Type all the indexing units in indexing order on the end opposite the key letter:
ACKERLY, David A.

▶ 3. Obtain appropriate color-coded labels for second and third letters of the first indexing unit:
A*CK*erly—White C on dark green background, White K on light brown background.

▶ 4. Attach labels to the file tab.

Figure 5-3

Alpha-Z Exercise

Neatly print the label below for each file folder as it would be typed and labeled. Also indicate which colors would be visible on the label. Use the coding as given in the text. Remember to indicate whether the letter or the background would be colored, i.e., Z, letter green; A, background red.

Austin State Junior College

Katherine Grant

Jeraldo Gerardo

Harold Zinkman

Reverend Caruthers

Variadex System

The files in this system are filed in alphabetic arrangement, but a color scheme is utilized on the guides for easy identification. Within each letter of the alphabet the colors orange, yellow, green, blue, and violet are used in that order.

One-fifth cut guides are staggered in the first and second positions for the alphabetic guides and miscellaneous secondary guides.

One-third cut folders are used in the second position for individual file folders.

Out folders and large-volume names or correspondence are identified with one-fifth cut guides in the fifth position.

Colored tabs are coded by the second letter of the first indexing unit:

1. Second letter a, b, c, d: orange;
2. Second letter e, f, g, h: yellow;
3. Second letter i, j, k, l, m, n: green;
4. Second letter o, p, q: blue;
5. Second letter r, s, t, u, v, w, x, y, z: violet.

These divisions then are seen in this respective order behind each primary letter guide. In addition, color strips or colored labels to correspond are used on the individual file folders.

Procedure

► 1. Identify first indexing unit and second letter of indexing unit: ACKERLY, C

► 2. Obtain appropriately color-coded label and type label in indexing order: ACKERLY, David A., orange

► 3. Attach label to second-position of a one-third cut file folder.

► 4. Locate appropriate secondary guide and file alphabetically behind other individual folders in that section.

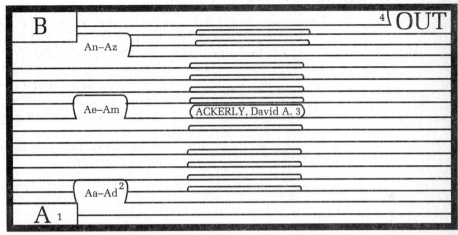

1— –First position, one–fifth cut alphabet guides

2— –Second position, one–fifth cut secondary guides

3— –Second position, one–third out individual, color–coded files

4— –Fifth position, one–fifth out out guides

Figure 5-4

Variadex Exercise

Neatly print the label below for each file folder as it would be typed and labeled. Also indicate which colors would be visible on the label. Use the coding as just given.

David Isaac Finklestein

Gerald Peter Swenson

Helen T. Raddison

Mark Thomas

Carolyn Marie Spalding

Harrison O. Bolton

Miscellaneous Color-Coded Systems

In addition to the specifically designed systems previously presented, many offices utilize color systems to meet their individuals needs. Following are some of the methods utilized.

Colored File Folders

One such system utilizes colored folders for first names, with the folders filed alphabetically by last name.

EXAMPLE: First name assigned color according to first letter.

A assigned red folders; G, green folders; S, blue folders:

Aaron Smith	Red folder	SMITH, Aaron
Aaron Hubert	Red folder	HUBERT, Aaron
Gloria Hansen	Green folder	HANSEN, Gloria
Susan Hansen	Blue folder	HANSEN, Susan
Susan Smith	Blue folder	SMITH, Susan

Many small offices utilize this system and find it quite effective. Obviously, in an office with a large volume, it would be a time-consuming method for locating files.

EXAMPLE: File folder assigned by first letter of last name.

S assigned pink folders, B assigned gray folders, M assigned orange folders:

Alice Smith	Pink folder	SMITH, Alice
Peter Sinclair	Pink folder	SINCLAIR, Peter
Allison Bothwell	Gray folder	BOTHWELL, Allison
Paul Mucheson	Orange folder	MUCHESON, Paul

This system makes it easy to spot folders that have been misfiled under an incorrect first letter, but does not provide further clues for misfilings within the first-letter guides.

Doctor Coding

In large clinics, this is a system used for identifying a particular doctor's files. Each doctor is assigned a particular color of folder. This allows for identification of folders that have been misfiled under the incorrect doctor, but the system is complicated when patients are seen by several doctors.

Color-Coding Numbers

This system is utilized in a numeric filing system. It operates in the same way that the alpha systems do. Numbers from 0 to 9 are color coded. The appropriate colored numbers are then placed on the tabs of the patient's folder.

EXAMPLE:

Through an accession record, David A. Ackerly has been assigned number 43668 and Adam D. Stevens number 47669.

Numbers have been assigned as follows: Orange, 1; pink, 2; green, 3; blue, 4; turquoise, 5; red, 6; brown, 7; yellow, 8; and purple, 9.

Ackerly Blue, green, red, red, yellow
Stevens Blue, brown, red, red, purple.

Thus, if Stevens' record were located right after Ackerly's, it could be easily spotted as being incorrectly filed because:

Blue, brown, red labels would not be consistent with
blue, green, red combination files on either side of it.

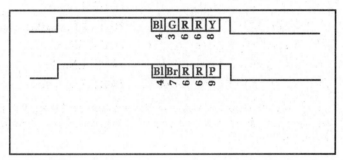

Figure 5-5

Numeric Color-Coding Exercise

Neatly print the label below for each file folder as it would be typed and labeled. Also indicate which colors would be visible on the label. Use the coding:

0, yellow; 1, red; 2, green; 3, blue; 4, violet; 5, orange; 6, brown; 7, black; 8, purple; and 9, turquoise.

Meredith Knapp, 83660

Presley Montana, 347

James Hudson, 54926

Ed Lyons, 3377

Hugh Wallner, 08

Assignment • 7

Take the list of names in Appendix C for the Color-Coding assignment. Appendix B contains color-coded labels.

Part A:

Using 3″ × 5″ cards or actual file folders, prepare the edge of the index cards or file folders as they would be assembled for actual office charts using the color-coded labels.

Part B:

Arrange the cards or folders in order by color system in the following order: Alpha-Z, numeric coloring, Tab-Alpha and Variadex.

UNIT 6

Numeric Filing

Objectives

1. Name the two major types of numeric filing systems.
2. Identify required elements of a numeric filing system.
3. Demonstrate the ability to file correctly using consecutive numbered filing.
4. Demonstrate the ability to file correctly using terminal digit filing.

Types of Numeric Filing Systems

- *Consecutive or Serial filing*—This system is commonly used in handling invoices, sales orders, requisitions, etc. Each record is numbered and filed in ascending order.
- *Nonconsecutive filing*—this system uses groups of two, three, or four digits, for example, social security numbers, phone numbers, etc., and is also called terminal digit filing.

When a numeric filing system is used, there are four essential components that you must have to utilize the system effectively. This applies to both a manual and a computerized system. The alphabetic card file and accession record in a manual system would be equivalent to the computerized record of the patient and whatever number is assigned to the patient in that computer record.

Components of the Numeric System

- *Serially Numbered Folders With Guides*

Items are consecutively numbered from lowest to highest, with numeric guides at intervals of 5, 10, etc., or 50, 100, etc.)

- *Alphabetic Miscellaneous Guides and Folders*

These are reserved for records that have not been assigned numbers. Correspondence is generally filed by subject or name in an alphabetic miscellaneous section, if there are only one or two items. When three pieces accumulate (the quantity may vary according to the office's policy), then a number is assigned. The miscellaneous folder is generally placed in front of all the numeric folders for ease of locating items.

- *Alphabetic Card File*

This is made up of cards containing name, address, and file number; cross reference here rather than in the number files.

This alphabetic file is necessary as a source for locating files or records. If you have laboratory data that comes into the office on Mary Wellington, you would need to know where to locate her chart in the numeric system in order to file the report.

This alphabetic file is kept in an index card fashion. In this file, then, you need to type the complete name and address (and any other information denoted by the office policy, for example, insurance, emergency numbers, etc.). Noted with this information there needs to be either an M (miscellaneous; for patients, clients, etc., not yet assigned a number) or an assigned number.

If a cross-reference is required, prepare a cross-reference card and include an X next to the number or M to indicate this is the cross-reference card, not the primary location.

```
                                                              #34500
  ┌────────────────────────────────────────┐
  │  PATIENT WITH ASSIGNED NUMBER           │
  └────────────────────────────────────────┘

  LASNETSKE, Robert Johann          Allentown Medical Ins
  7829 NW Platoon Drive             Policy #788-23-44082
  Bangor, WA  98315                 Group #5428
  H Phone:  285-2308
  W Phone:  778-0231
```

```
                                                                   M
  ┌────────────────────────────────────────┐
  │  FILE LOCATED IN MISCELLANEOUS          │
  └────────────────────────────────────────┘

  Allenmore Medical Center
  3358 Yakina Avenue
  Sweetwater, WA  98308
```

Figure 6-1 *Alphabetic card file: (top) with number; (bottom) number not assigned.*

```
                                                         #99082 – X



  BLACKENWALD, Kit              DSHS Coupons
  358 Lebo Drive SW                                                6-2
  Frontier, Tx  77029



  SEE       BLACKENWALD, Reginald
```

Figure 6-2 *Cross-reference card*

- *Accession Record*

This record is some type of journal where numbers are preassigned: Each new item to be assigned is written on the line next to the number. Each new entry for which a chart will be created must be assigned a number. A computerized system would have an accession record in its memory bank.

#	File Name
ACCESSION LOG BOOK	
800	LAWSON, Sarah
801	SMITH, Fred
802	TREMONT Drug Supply
803	Mandelson, Trixie
804	
805	
808	
807	

Figure 6-3

Filing Procedures with a Numeric System

- Inspect and index the item to be filed using alphabetic rules and procedures, including release marks and tickler notations.
- Code for filing units. The first unit in the "filing label" to be coded is underlined and subsequent units are numbered.

	2	3			2	3
<u>Warren</u>	Leslie	Aileen		A1	Office	Supplies

- Cross-reference. Draw a double wavy line under the first unit, and place an X in the top, right-hand corner. Remember the cross-reference is filed *only in the alphabetic card file.*

	2	**3**
Warren-Beatty	Jennifer	Sue

with cross-reference card

	2	**3**		**X**	**2**	**3**
Beatty ~~~ ~~~	Jennifer	Sue	SEE	Warren-Beatty	Jennifer	Sue

- Sort according to the first coded unit and arrange in sections for ease of filing.
- Check the alphabetic card file for each piece to see if the card has already been prepared.
  1. Write the number in the upper right-hand corner if it has been assigned a number.
  2. If no number is assigned, check the miscellaneous file (M) to see if there are enough documents in that file to assign a number. If there are, make a card and note the number in the right-hand corner of the card file, cross out the M, and make a chart file; if there is an insufficient number, continue to code the document with an M.
  3. If there is no card, make up an alphabetic card, as follows:
     (a) Complete the name and address.
     (b) Write either M or assign a number.
     (c) Cross reference if necessary.
     (d) File the card properly.
- File the document in the appropriate file folder/chart.

Consecutive Filing

Files under this system are simply filed in ascending order. The miscellaneous folder is placed in front of all the numbered file(s). This is the most optimum place for the file(s) for two reasons: (1) You do not have to continue to reorder items each time a numbered file is added to the back of the order, and (2) In a large system of files, retrieval in the front would be quick and easy.

FILED: Miscellaneous, 1, 2, 33, 86, 101, 940, 1103

Nonconsecutive Filing (Terminal Digit)

In this filing system, numbers are grouped and arranged in ascending order using the far right, or terminal digits. Each group of numbers is considered a unit (one number). The number of digits in a group does not have to be consistent; again, the group is considered one unit.

INDEXING ORDER			1st	2nd	3rd
2108	23	879	879	23	2108
9800	233	23	23	233	9800
98	2382	1	1	2382	98

To file the terminal digit files in numerical order, you consider strictly the *terminal digit unit*. If two of those are identical, proceed to compare the next set of digits. If the first and second units are identical, proceed to the third, and so on.

FILE NUMBER		
123	11	8099
1098	2	808
1083	111	808
098	11	8099
193	13	998
578	06	5983

IN ORDER			
1.	1098	2	808
2.	1083	111	808
3.	193	13	998
4.	578	06	5983
5.	098	11	8099
6.	123	11	8099

Assignment • 8

Part A:

Type the names found in Appendix C for the numeric filing assignment in proper indexing order on 3″ × 5″ cards. Code the cards as described in the text.

Part B:

File the cards by *terminal digit filing order* and list the proper order on the sheet of paper for Assignment 8.

Part C:

File the cards by *consecutive filing order* and list the proper order on a sheet of paper for Assignment 8. You will ignore the spaces between the groups of numbers and treat the numbers as one unit.

Soundex (Phonetic) Filing

Objectives

1. State the uses of a subject filing system in a health care facility.
2. Identify required elements of a subject filing system.
3. Index and code materials for filing by subject.

This system is not widely used because it requires somewhat extensive training in order to learn the coding methods. However, a number of large medical facilities utilize it. Therefore, an introduction to it will prepare you, at a minimum, to understand the method that is utilized.

In medical offices, particularly, there are a great many variations of name spellings. Therefore, files can easily become misfiled and/or difficult to locate. This is an especially critical problem in a medical setting, where location of files must be a timely process. For instance, if a pharmacy calls in for verification of a prescription or an emergency long-distance call is received requesting information on a patient named "Christiansen," how do you locate the patient's file quickly and efficiently? Let's assume that the party on the phone does not know the exact spelling. Is it Christiansen? Christensen? Christenson? Cristiansen? Or you may receive records from another clinic and find the handwriting so sloppy throughout the records that you are unable to determine the accurate spelling of the patient's name.

The Soundex system groups names phonetically regardless of the spellings. The key indexing unit is the surname of an individual or the first coded unit of a name.

- This unit is given a code consisting of one letter and three digits:

> | | |
> |---|---|
> | Torkelson | First letter + three number digits |

- The letter in the code is the first letter of the key unit, and the three digits are numbers that are assigned to certain consonants in the surname or key unit (see Procedure #_____:

> | | |
> |---|---|
> | Torkelson | T + 6 for R, 2 for C, and 4 for L |

- Once the key unit has been coded utilizing the phonetics, the filing order is then determined by the alphanumeric code.

> | | |
> |---|---|
> | Torkelson | Filed under T section, then 624 would follow T623 |

In the case of identical code numbers with the first indexing unit, just as in alphabetic filing, the order is determined by the second unit. Similarly, if the second units are identical the third and successive units are utilized.

> Torkelson, Jane (T624, Jane)
>
> would come before
>
> Torkelson, Matthew (T624, Matthew)

Pros and Cons of the Phonetic Method:

As with a numeric system, every name has only one number. This speeds up sorting, filing, and locating files. So, too, family names are automatically grouped. This would make finding files of siblings, or parents/siblings quicker. Rather than coding for the entire alphabet, only seven letters need to be used. Additionally, files from other systems can easily be converted to this filing method.

On the flip side, it is time consuming to learn phonetic coding. You may encounter problems with retrieval of files if they are improperly coded. *Cross-referencing is not used*, which can, therefore, make certain files difficult to locate.

Procedure

▶ 1. Phonetic filing is accomplished by dropping vowels (Jhnsn for Johnson) and coding similar-sounding consonants:

Key Letters	Code Numbers	Equivalents
B	1	P F V
C	2	S K G J Q X Z
D	3	T
L	4	None
M	5	N
R	6	None

▶ 2. To code for Soundex, the initial letter of the name is retained as spelled. *Note:* W and H are dropped entirely except as initial letters.

Orwetz is coded: O + r, t, z
Stehmanson is coded: S + t, m, n
Hipilito is coded: H + p, l, t

▶ 3. If two of the same key letters, or a key letter and its equivalent, are separated by a, e, i, o, u or y, code separately.

Hillsken is coded: H + l, s, k
Trililofson: T + r, l, l
Bemmerson: B + m, r, s
Domamaski: D + m, m, s

▶ 4. If two of the same key letters, or a key letter and its equivalent, are separated by h or w, code as one letter.

a dwd combination would use d and d

whereas

a dd combination would use just one d

▶ 5. After the initial letter, a name is coded up to three characters.

Yanagimachi: Y + n, g, m
Wormsley: W + r, m, s
Wozniak: W + z, n, k

▶ 6. Zeros are added when necessary to complete three digits.

Yekel: W + k, l, 0
Yee: Y + 0, 0, 0

NAME	ELIMINATE	KEY LETTERS	ALPHANUMERIC CODE
Salveson	a, e	S + L + B(v) + C(s)	S412 L = 4, B = 1, C = 2
St. Clair	——	S + D(t) + C + L	S324 D = 3, C = 2, L = 4
Christiansen	h, i	C + R + C(s) + D(t)	C623 R = 6, C = 2, D = 3
Christensen	h, i	C + R + C(s) + D(t)	C623 R = 6, C = 2, D = 3
Cristianson	i	C + R + C(s) + D(t)	C623 R = 6, C = 2, D = 3

You can see by this illustration that the "Christiansen" file could be much more quickly located by the C623 filing than by trying all of the variations of the name spellings.

Filing of Phonetic Files/Indexing Cards

1. File all names beginning with the initial letter behind the main letter guide.

Lewiston behind L   Monroe behind M

2. Files are then located behind left-hand/first position guides according to groupings of key letters of the surname, or first indexing unit coded along with coded numbers for those groupings.

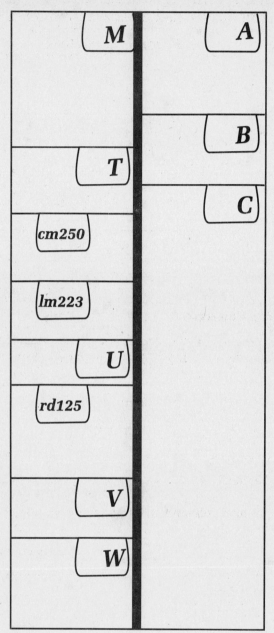

Figure 7-1 *Soundex main and secondary guides*

KEY LTRS/CODES	SURNAME	CODING LTRS	KEY LETTERS
s mcl 524	Shanklin	ShaNKL	N = M, K = C, L
md 530	Schmidt	SchMDt	M, D, 0 (DT as one letter) (add 0 for third)
T cm 250	Tyson	TySoN	S = C, N = M, 0 (SN as two, sepa- rated by vowel) (add 0 for third)
mc 520	Thomas	ThoMaS	M, S = C, 0 (add 0 for third)
rm 650	Thurman	ThuRMn	R, M, 0 (MN as one letter) (add 0 for third)

Soundex Filing Exercise

In the right-hand column identify the letters that would be used in the coding process in order to arrive at an alphanumeric filing code:

Spelled	*Letters Used in Coding*
Peter Robinson	_____
Doctor Robison	_____
Samuel Robinsson	_____
Alice De Roberson	_____
Alice Robertson	_____

In the right-hand column list the alphanumeric filing code for each of the given names/organizations:

Spelled	*Alphanumeric Filing Code*
Fifth Avenue Boutique	_____
George Samuelson	_____
Abbey Mill-Aims	_____
St. Joseph's Academy	_____
Phillip DeMorris	_____

Assignment • 9

On a piece of paper labeled Assignment 9, match the following names with the proper secondary guide found below:

Name

Martin

Davis

Lahammer

Pfitzer

Klinker

Tiner

Kopel

Morden

Jacobsen

Lomax

Secondary Guides:

rdm 635	bc 120	lmc 452
bdc 132	mr 560	kpl 140
bl 140	rtm 635	cbc 21
mc 520	ftz 132	pl 140

8

SUBJECT FILING

Objectives

1. Explain how a subject filing system would be used in a health care facility.
2. Identify the steps used in subject filing.
3. Organize information files using a subject filing system.

There are many reasons why material would be filed using a system of subjects in a medical office. The doctor doing research might wish to index it according to diseases. Subject files would be a convenient way of locating types of services you frequently use or for which you provide references to patients. Also, information that you receive from different types of insurance companies might be filed by subject.

When using a subject system, you must scan the material to determine the topic or theme. As with numeric filing, you need an *alphabetic file*. This can be either a list or an *index card file listing the subjects*. Also, as with numeric filing, all cross-reference cards are done only with the alphabetic file listings.

Within the folders, material is arranged alphabetically. For instance, if using subject indexing for research projects which the doctor is conducting, you would need to identify the subject category, and then in the material, code an item for reference to that specific material:

Procedure

SUBJECT: Toxic Exposure
CODE: Patient name.

Steps to Follow In Indexing:

- Review the item in order to find the subject.
- Match the subject of the item with an appropriate category on the subject index list.
- If the item contains information that may pertain to more than one subject, decide on the proper cross-reference.

Steps to Follow In Coding:

- If the subject title is written on the material, underline it.
- If the subject title is not written on the item, write it clearly in the upper right-hand corner and underline it.
- Use a wavy line for cross-referencing and an X, as with alphabetic and numeric filing.
- Underline the first indexing unit of the coded unit(s).

Figure 8-1

PHONE REFILL REQUEST *SUBJECT: PHONE REFILLS*

PATIENT *Wallner, Marilyn E. (IKR 8/17/72)*   X–Wallner, Marilyn E.

TIME/DATE *10:15 a.m.*   *August 24*

DRUG *Percocet*

DATE OF LAST REFILL *August 1, 80 tablets*

APPROVED ☐ **DENIED** ☒

TIME/DATE PT ADVISED *9:10 p.m. August, 24—00 refills until 9/01*

Dr. Boncowski has a PHONE REFILL file which he uses to track opiate refill prescriptions. An appropriate cross reference would be the patient's personal file where a notation should be charted.

Figure 8-2

PHONE REFILL REQUEST   X–Wallner, Marilyn E.

PATIENT *Wallner, Marilyn E. (IKR 8/17/72)*

TIME/DATE *10:15 a.m.*   *August, 24*

DRUG *Percocet*

DATE OF LAST REFILL *August 1, 80 tablets*

APPROVED ☐ **DENIED** ☒

TIME/DATE PT ADVISED *9:10 p.m. August 24—00 refills until 9/01*

Dr. Boncowski has a PHONE REFILL file which he uses to track opiate refill prescriptions. An appropriate cross reference would be the patient's personal file where a notation should be charted.

Assignment • 10

In Doctor Saunders' office, his receptionist, Claudean, has decided to organize the business files. The office constantly receives materials and flyers from various companies. Claudean would like a way to be able to retrieve this information in a quick and efficient manner. She has, therefore, decided to use subject files in which she has names and addresses as well as pertinent flyers from those organizations.

In Appendix B you will find the tab guides of the subjects Claudean has chosen to use. In Appendix C there is a list of the agencies the office will be dealing with. You are to set up a mini filing system as follows:

1. List each agency on a 3″ × 5″ card.
2. File the guides in alphabetic order.
3. File in alphabetic order all materials behind the subject guides.
4. Answer the following questions regarding the filed cards. List the answers on a separate sheet of paper for comparison with the teacher's guide.
    (a) How many cards are filed under Office Supplies?
    (b) What agencies did you cross reference? What subject(s) were they cross-referenced under?
    (c) For which agencies did you need to use the address rule in order to file them in proper order?
    (d) What is the proper order (from first to last behind the subject) of the agencies filed under Pharmaceutical Companies and Representatives?
    (e) Illustrate how you cross-referenced one of the agencies. Show both the main file card and the cross-reference file card.

UNIT 9

Geographic Filing

Objectives

1. Explain how a geographic filing system would be used in a health care facility.
2. Identify the steps used in geographic filing.
3. Organize patient files for an epidemiological study.

This filing system is used most often in the medical setting where the doctor or clinic is doing research or is involved in infectious disease. Very simply, the primary guides are states, counties, towns, etc. Secondary guides are identified units that break down the primary units into smaller ones.

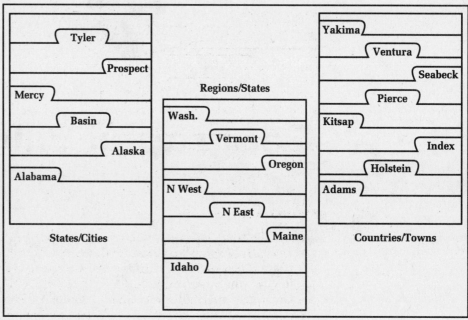

Figure 9-1 *Primary and secondary guides*

Procedure

- Take steps as for alphabetic filing procedures—inspect, index, code, and cross-reference if required.
- If the material is on letterhead and the letterhead shows more than one address, the original piece is filed under the most important address with a cross-reference for the other, as would be the case if the parent company is located in New York and correspondence is received from the Los Angeles office.
- Sort by primary unit and then by secondary guide topics. Each primary topic has a primary guide with the tab in the first position and a miscellaneous folder with a tab in the last position. A primary miscellaneous folder is used for materials that do not yet have individual folders.
- Place individual folders for secondary topics between the primary guide and the miscellaneous folder.

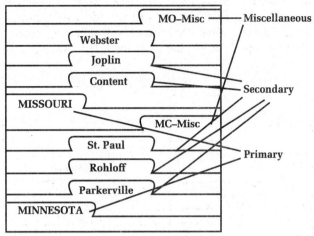

Figure 9-2 *City/state/ miscellaneous guides*

Assignment • 11

Doctor Whitman is involved in epidemiological research in the field of multiple sclerosis. The doctor has compiled a list of current patients who have been officially diagnosed as having the disease. Using a geographic system, file the patients found in Appendix C for the geographic filing exercise. Primary and secondary guide labels are located in Appendix B.

Make a 3″ × 5″ card for each patient, including all the information provided. A miscellaneous folder will not be used, as Doctor Whitman needs to identify all locations individually.

Part A:

1. Set up the primary and secondary guide using the "A" labels (i.e., New York-A, Washington-A, Albany-A).
2. File the patients geographically according to their place of birth.
3. On a piece of paper, list the filing order of these cards.

    EXAMPLE: Kentucky: Louisville—Brown, Smith
    Sweetwater—Klinger, Stapeski
    Tennessee: Knoxville—Sanders, Bartrum

Part B:

1. Remove all of the patient cards from the geographic files.
2. Set up a new get of primary and secondary guides using the "B" labels.

3. Select *only* the cards of Doctor Whitman's patients who resided in Washington, Oregon, or Idaho for more than five years up until age ten.

4. File these cards in geographic order according to the place the patients resided for the majority of the first ten years of their life.

5. List on the paper used in Part A the filing order of these cards.

10

Correspondence Filing Procedures

Objectives

1. Distinguish incoming from outgoing correspondence.
2. Demonstrate the ability to code and index materials to be filed.
3. Process correspondence using release marks and filing in alphabetic order.

Correspondence is processed as outlined in the filing procedures unit using alphabetic filing rules. However, an additional step is necessary in identifying incoming versus outgoing correspondence. The steps for filing correspondence are as outlined below.

Inspection

For filing purposes, correspondence must be filed by a system that will make it distinctly identifiable, i.e., utilizing the label that would most likely be thought of if someone wanted to retrieve that correspondence (or file additional relevant correspondence). In this process, the correspondence must be identified as either *incoming* or *outgoing*.

Incoming Correspondence

Incoming correspondence is defined as that which is received *into* the office from an outside source. This type of correspondence would be filed under the most important name—the most likely name by which someone would retrieve it. The key place to look is *the letterhead* or *patient or item referenced in the letter*.

Outgoing Correspondence

Similarly, correspondence being sent *out* of your office is considered the outgoing correspondence. The key element here is the *inside address* or the *patient or item referenced in the letter*. Again, remember that you want to identify the most probable place for locating the correspondence should you need it for future use.

At this point inspect to see if the item is ready to be filed— that is, that all appropriate action has been taken. If not, take care of copies, enclosures, and note in the tickler file for future action, as required, before proceeding with the indexing.

It is a good practice to use some type of release mark on every piece of correspondence, whether or not action is required. Ideally the doctor initials the document after reading it. Then if action is required on the part of the medical assistant/medical secretary, a release mark is in a consistently identified place on every document after the appropriate action has been completed. If no action is required, after the doctor has signed outgoing correspondence or initialed incoming correspondence, place the release mark on the document. A release mark on every piece of correspondence serves as an excellent quality-control measure.

Indexing

Incoming Correspondence

- Be sure that the letterhead is related to the letter.
- When both the company name and the signature are important, index the company name.
- If there is no letterhead and you have determined that the material is not relevant to a patient's chart, index the name on the signature line.
- **Caution**: Be sure that the letterhead is related to the letter. For instance, a personal letter written on hotel stationery or drug company sample stationery would not be relevant to the letterhead.

Outgoing Correspondence

Look at the inside address and the reference line.

- If the correspondence is relevant to a patient, that would be your indexing guideline.
- Otherwise, you would look to the inside address for indexing information. When the inside address is relevant and contains both a company name and a person's name, index the company name (this avoids the problem of personnel changes); cross-referencing would be done under the individual name.
- If the letter is personal, the name of the person to whom the letter is written would be used for indexing purposes.

Coding

- Code the indexing units of the designated label.
- If the correspondence is being cross-referenced be sure to note the cross-referencing unit and place the X in a visible place. You may find that the body of the letter contains an important name, subject, or the like. If it is possible that a piece of correspondence may be referred to in the future by more than one indexing label, prepare a cross-reference.
- If you code the correspondence in the upper right hand corner, this will save you time when an item is retrieved and then refiled.

Allan Hoblin
6799 East Ohio St.
Upper Sandusky, OH.

AAFP– –April Seminar

January 31, 1992

William Salter, M.D.
5360 Pacific Avenue
Kaiser, OR 97405

Dear Dr. Salter,

I am writing to inquire as to whether you will be attending the
April seminar of the family physicians. We would appreciate
it very much if you could speak to us regarding your recent trip
to the clinic in Nicaragua. I understand you have some interesting
tales to relate regarding the children in the villages you served.

Please contact my office at 509-345-0828. My secretary can
relay the information to me. Thank you for your consideration.

Sincerely,

Allan Hoblin, M.D.
AH/ldz

By coding you do not have to guess where it went last time or where a similar letter might be found.

Figure 10-1

Filing

- Sort through the items to be filed and separate into alphabetic, color-coded, numeric, etc. piles if there are a number of items to be sorted.
- Place all papers in the file with their letterhead or code at the top. If the individual folder is not set up in sub-units (see Appendix D), file according to the date, with the most recent item on top. (The top is what you see first when you open the folder.)
- *Remember to check for a release mark.*

- For correspondence, a miscellaneous folder is created for items that do not number enough (office policy dictates: anywhere from two to four pieces) to warrant an individual folder. Items in the miscellaneous folder are filed alphabetically first, and then identical items are filed with the most recent piece on top. An individual folder is then created when enough pieces accumulate on a particular item.
- Remove paper clips, and staple items together.
- Place documents in appropriate folders and cross-reference the files.

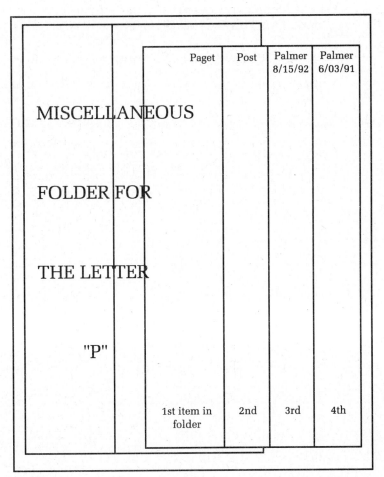

Figure 10-2 *A miscellaneous folder*

The same steps are followed with any type of correspondence. If you are using a subject filing system, the identified subject would be coded in the top right-hand corner on each piece of correspondence. Using a geographic system, the coding would either be noted in the top right-hand corner or it could be circled or outlined if the location appears in the correspondence.

Assignment • 12

In Appendix C you will find 20 pieces of correspondence associated with Doctor Sheridan's office. You are to set up the files using one of the color-coding systems or a numeric system, using either actual file folders or a cardboard or heavy paper dividers. Blank labels are provided in Appendix B. Process all of the correspondence, from inspecting through filing. Be sure to make 3″ × 5″ cards for any tickler items, arranging them by date and placing a rubber band around them. If you use a numeric system, you will need an alpha card file and accession record as well. Turn in the completed set of files and any accessory items.

UNIT 11

Record Retention

Objectives

1. Discuss the process of purging files.
2. Identify general rules for storage of records.
3. Distinguish between microfiche, microfilm, and jackets.
4. State reasons for filming records.

Health care facilities store information in individual, easily accessible charts. As the health information accumulates and the size of files grows, it is necessary to maintain the files by the process known as purging. Terms associated with this process are:

- *Active Files*—Those records that need to be readily accessible for retrieval of information.

- *Inactive Files*—Those records that need to be retained for possible retrieval of information. Files not currently being accessed for information would thus become inactive. Often, the type of practice will dictate the relevant time period after which files are determined to be inactive (generally two to three years).

- *Files to be Destroyed*—Files that are no longer required. Increasingly, patient files are retained for significantly longer periods of time due to litigation and research considerations.

- *Record purging*—Simply stated, this means cleaning out the files.

The purging process requires sorting through the records and removing those not in active use. Each facility should establish a standard policy for control and processing of records. States have different time requirements for retention of various types of records (see Table 11-1 for samples). With the abundance of medical litigation, a greater number of facilities are choosing to maintain large inactive files rather than destroy the records. You should check with the Medical Practice Act in the state of your health care facility to determine record-keeping requirements.

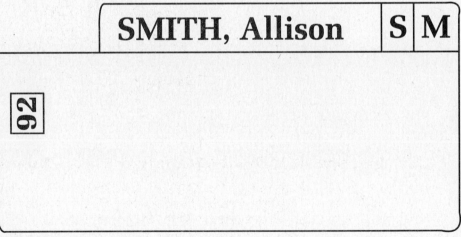

Figure 11-1 *A year-coded file*

In small health care facilities, the most common method of purging patient files is to affix a year-dated sticker to a visible portion of the patient chart. (Figure 11-1) When a patient returns, if the year-dated sticker on the chart is not current, a current-year sticker is affixed to the chart. This system allows the office personnel to scan the files visually on a predetermined schedule in order to remove the inactive files. These records are generally stored either on site or in an off-site facility where security can be maintained. There are available firms that specialize in storing medical records.

In large institutions, purging must be done on a very regular basis as the volume of information quickly increases. Therefore, large clinics and hospitals use microfiche, microfilm, and film jackets to store inactive and/or closed records.

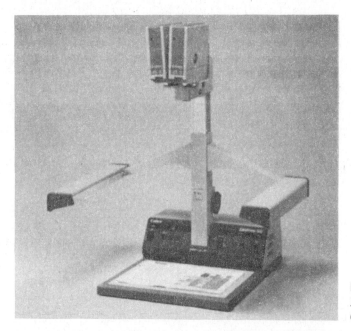

Figure 11-2 *Microfilm Machine (Courtesy of Canon, Inc.)*

Process of Converting Records to Film (Courtesy of Canon, Inc.)

Figure 11-2 illustrates how these records are converted from hard copy to film. The document is placed on the table in appropriate camera range. The camera, which is equipped with lighting equipment, is located overhead. The process of filming proceeds in a manner similar to using a common photocopy machine. Once the records are on film, originals can be destroyed as they have been reproduced in their entirety.

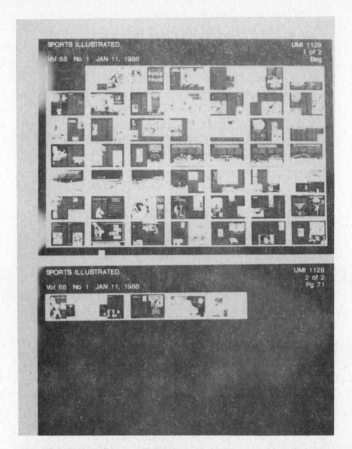

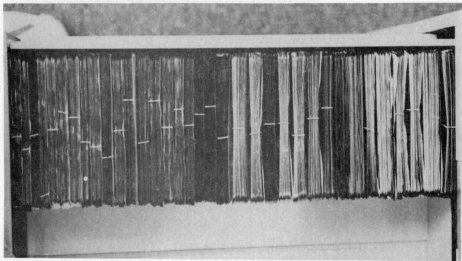

Figure 11-3 *Microfiche Files*

Microfiche files (Figure 11-3) allow for storage of miniaturized records on 3″ × 5″ cards. These plastic sheets of cards are stored in drawers much as you would find index cards in a library file. These systems require some type of indexing system to locate the individual records, as well as special equipment to view the films.

Microfiche files are filed by number. The number is located on the top, right-hand corner of the 3″ × 5″ sheet. The sheet is viewed by placing it in a special video display machine, which magnifies the material so it can be read easily. Figure 11-4 shows a machine that can read the "fiche" files and make a copy of them.

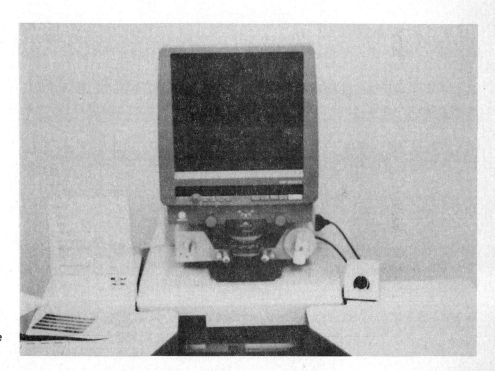

Figure 11-4 *Microfiche reader and printer*

Microfilm utilizes a process whereby records are filmed and stored as rolls of film. A microfilm roll can hold considerably more records than one microfiche card. However, the bulky rilm rolls require more storage space (Figure 11-5).

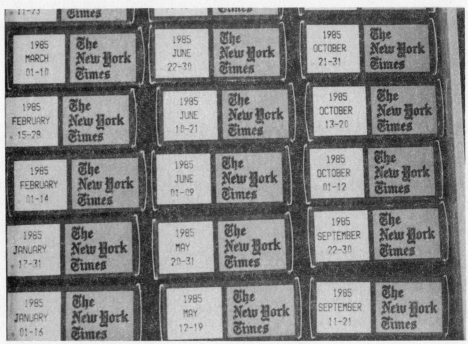

Figure 11-5 *Microfilm rolls*

Microfilm files are usually kept in a box labeled with the file's contents. The labeling of these boxes could be accomplished using a number of methods. For instance, a large hospital might microfilm the records of one patient on a single roll of film if that patient had an extensive set of files. Or a roll of film might contain files on patients BDI-ECK, covering the dates of April 1, 1986–May 1, 1986.

Records within rolls are usually identified by page numbers. Thus, if you were trying to locate a file on Henry R. Levine who was seen on April 19, 1986, you would review the indexing record to locate both the number of the microfilm roll and the page number within that roll of film. The records could then be located and viewed. Some machines are equipped with a copier, so that when you have located the file, or particular information within that file, you can then simply photocopy the information directly off the roll of microfilm (Figure 11-6).

Figure 11-6 *Microfilm reader printer (courtesy of Canon, Inc.)*

Jackets refer to individual records that have been filmed. The film is then converted to a flat medium by cutting the roll and placing the film into jacket folders for individual patients. This is a process regularly used in radiology facilities where the flat films are stored as patient charts.

Table 11-1 RECORDS FOR RETENTION

Patient Index Files These include appointment books and are kept for an indefinite period of time. They may be required for litigation and/or research.

Case Histories The length of storage depends on state requirements and individual practice requirements. Product liability cases have made long-term storage of these records mandatory (20+ years). Minors' records must be retained until the age of majority, at a minimum.

If records are to be destroyed owing to the death of a physician or closure of a practice, the following procedure is required: Each patient should be notified of the circumstances and given the opportunity to have his or her records forwarded to another physician. After notification, the records must be retained for a "reasonable" period of time (determined by state regulations). A period of three to six months is generally determined to be a "reasonable" period of time. The records must then be destroyed by burning or shredding to protect confidentiality.

Personal Records Professional licenses should be stored permanently in a secure location.

Office Equipment Records These records are generally kept until the warranties and/or depreciation are no longer valid. They should be kept in an easily accessible location if equipment is under maintenance contract.

Insurance Records Professional liability policies are kept permanently. Other policies are kept in active files while in force.

Financial records Bank records are kept in active files for up to three years and then placed in inactive storage. Tax records must be retained permanently.

Laboratory and X-ray Data Originals should be retained permanently with the patient's case history.

12

Computers and Database Files

Objectives

1. Explain the uses for database files in health care facilities.
2. Identify the terms used to set up databases.
3. Demonstrate procedures to set up database files.

Computer-Related Files

In a health care facility, individual patient charts must be maintained in order to file actual health information pertaining to the care of the patient. However, computer files can be a very useful tool in maintaining and processing related information.

There are a number of software programs specifically designed for the medical setting. These are most frequently used to manage bookkeeping, insurance forms, and appointment scheduling. However, they can also be used to maintain files of information in what is called a database. Many of these specialized programs can be used for database functions, but popular programs such as Excel, dBase, FoxPro, and Microsoft Works allow you to create your own databases.

What is a Database?

Simply put, a database is a worksheet consisting of *records that contain categories of information*. In a health care setting you might use a database to:

- Maintain a list of patients
- Determine the number of times a particular procedure is performed
- Categorize patients by age, sex, etc.
- Organize treatment data for research
- Notify patients of a drug recall
- Create a list of specialists for patient care
- Create an inventory supply list
- Compile data on patients with a particular type of insurance

Databases allow you to access bases (or files of information) quickly. For instance, if a physician needs to notify patients of a drug recall, the staff could search the records of patients who are taking the medication. Conducting this task by hand would be time consuming and allows for the possibility that some patients could be missed. However, if all patients on any type of medication were listed in a database, a search could be conducted for records containing the recall drug. The doctor could quickly arrive at a list (or group of records) consisting of patients on the recall drug and immediately create a new database.

These databases can be as simple or as complex as the task requires. You can use the information to count, calculate, and summarize data. Thus, databases are particularly useful in a large clinical or hospital setting. The reports can be only straight facts as in a computer printout, or they can be "dressed up" to be used for a presentation.

How Do You Create a Database?

Terms

- *Field Labels*: Labels that define fields.
  Last name
- *Fields*: Individual items in a record.
  Jenkins
- *Record*: All of the information associated with one particular name (patient, hospital, disease)

Name:	Jenkins, Floyd	SS#: 567-29-3329
F Name:	3632 8th Street	
Address:	Akron,	
	Kansas	Zip: 67156
DOB:	3-02-65	

- *Report (Database)*: All of the individual records that were created.
      105 records on active patients = one database
      22 records on inactive patients = one database

Procedure

Regardless of the type of program you are utilizing, you will follow the same basic steps to create a database:

▶ 1. Design a form by defining (labeling) the fields. Figure 12-1

▶ 2. Enter individual data into fields for each record in the database. Figure 12-2

▶ 3. Customize the database form by adding titles, creating groupings, changing column widths, making labels in italics or bold, centering text, etc. Figure 12-3

▶ 4. Give the database a report name and save for future use. Fogire 12-4

Once the database has been created, you can use it to view, edit, summarize, search, group, copy, or print the information. You can even transfer the database information into word processing documents to save time required in keyboarding the information again.

Let us say that your physician has just received information on a new experimental drug approved for use by parkinsonian patients over age 60 and wants you to type a letter to send to those particular patients. You can therefore use your database program to retrieve the patient list database, select the parkinsonian patients over age 60, and create a new database to use for your mailing list.

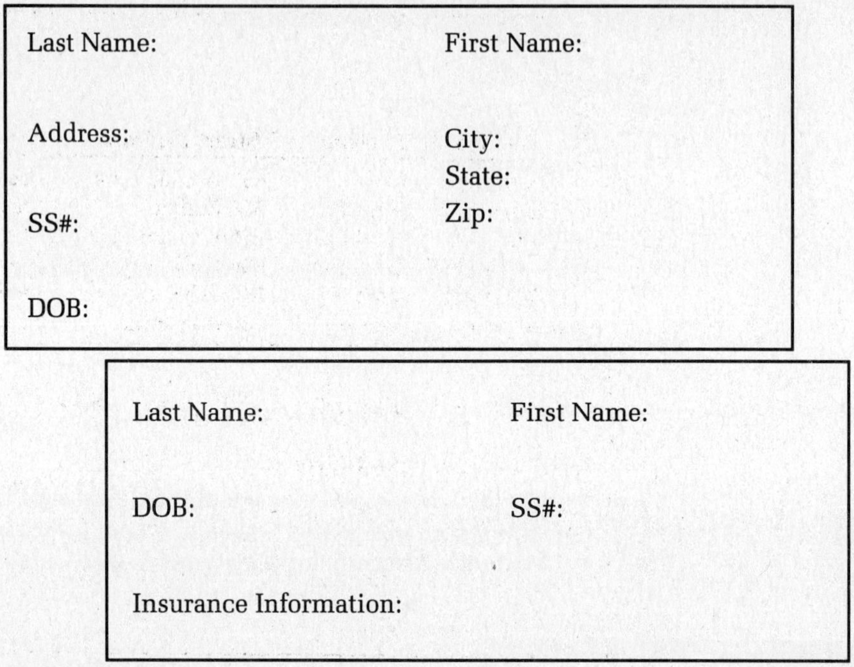

Last Name: First Name:

Address: City:
                                   State:
SS#:   Zip:

DOB:

Last Name: First Name:

DOB: SS#:

Insurance Information:

Figure 12-1 *Two database forms*

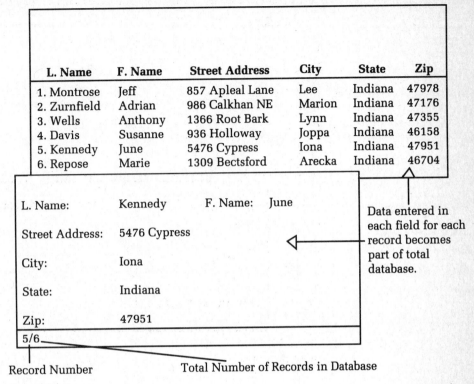

L. Name	F. Name	Street Address	City	State	Zip
1. Montrose	Jeff	857 Apleal Lane	Lee	Indiana	47978
2. Zurnfield	Adrian	986 Calkhan NE	Marion	Indiana	47176
3. Wells	Anthony	1366 Root Bark	Lynn	Indiana	47355
4. Davis	Susanne	936 Holloway	Joppa	Indiana	46158
5. Kennedy	June	5476 Cypress	Iona	Indiana	47951
6. Repose	Marie	1309 Bectsford	Arecka	Indiana	46704

L. Name: Kennedy   F. Name: June

Street Address: 5476 Cypress

City: Iona

State: Indiana

Zip: 47951

5/6

Data entered in each field for each record becomes part of total database.

Record Number

Total Number of Records in Database

Figure 12-2

ACTIVE PATIENT LIST

L. Name	F. Name	Street Address	City	State	Zip
1. Montrose	Jeff	857 Aplael Lane	Lee	Indiana	47978
2. Zurnfield	Adrian	986 Callahan NE	Marion	Indiana	47176
3. Wells	Anthony	1366 Root Bark	Lynn	Indiana	47355
4. Davis	Susanne	936 Holloway	Joppa	Indiana	46158
5. Kennedy	June	5476 Cypress	Iona	Indiana	47951
6. Repose	Marie	1309 Bedsford	Arecka	Indiana	46704

Figure 12-3

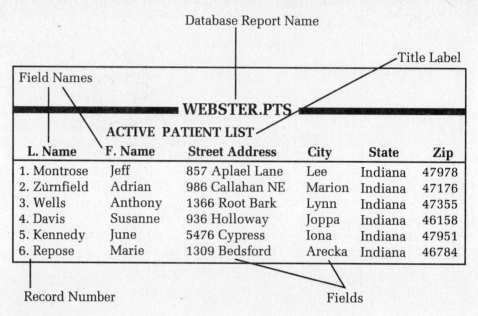

Figure 12-4

Assignment • 13

This assignment is designed for those classrooms equipped with computers and with access to a database management program.

1. Using Doctor Whitman's list of patients in Appendix C, labeled Assignment 13, *create a database* for the patients with multiple sclerosis. You may set the form up in any order you wish. *Design the form* using the following fields:

Last name	First name
Sex	Age
Street Address*	City*
State*	Zip Code*
Birthplace**	Where Raised***

   * Information is the current address, state, zip.
   ** List cities spelled out and abbreviations for states.
   *** List the state abbreviations only.

3. *Produce a printout* of the MS patient list, making sure the report printout has a title. You may edit the labeling, columns, etc. as you wish.

4. *Search the MS patient list* for Dr. Whitman's MS patients over the age of 30. *Create a new database* and *produce a printout* of these patients.

APPENDIX **A**

Alpha Self-Study Keys
Alpha Filing Rules

Self-Study Keys

Patient Chart Filing

A. NAME	PROPER INDEXING ORDER
1. Diane V. (LN) Brown	Brown, Diane V
2. Edgar A. (LN Allen) St. Leason	Stleason, Edgar Allen
3. Cullen Thomas di Salvo	Disalvo, Cullen Thomas
4. Mandy-Louise T. (LN Teresa) Dawson	Dawson, Mandylouise Teresa
5. Larry (LN Lawrence) P (LN) Brocerick-O'Reilly	Brocerickoreilly, Lawrence P
6. Ned Parker McAdams	Mcadams, Ned Parker
7. Chuck (LN) Al (LN Albert) Trevontaine	Trevontaine, Chuck Albert
8. Jean-Marie Saint Vincent	Saintvincent, Jeanmarie
9. Dr. Herbert Brown	Brown, Herbert Dr
10. Ann-Marie Sue (LN Suzanne) Tochitti	Tochitti, Annmarie Suzanne

B. CORRECT ALPHABETIC ORDER

1. Brocerickoreilly
2. Brown, Diane
3. Brown, Herbert
4. Dawson
5. Disalvo
6. Mcadams
7. Saintvincent
8. Stleason
9. Tochitti
10. Trevontaine

Alpha Filing, Rules 1-3

A. NAME	PROPER INDEXING ORDER
Gene Custer	Custer, Gene
R. Allan Quigley	Quigley, R Allan
Susan Marie Jones	Jones, Susan Marie
Stephen P. Pfeiffer	Pfeiffer, Stephen P
A. S. Stevens	Stevens, A S

Brady Allan Jones	Jones, Brady Allan
Thomas Edward Brady	Brady, Thomas Edward
George B. Shaw	Shaw, George B
Robert Chuck Adams	Adams, Robert Chuck
Debra Louise Lindquist	Lindquist, Debra Louise

B. PROPER ALPHABETIC ORDER

1. Adams
2. Brady
3. Custer
4. Jones, Brady
5. Jones, Susan
6. Lindquist
7. Pfeiffer
8. Quigley
9. Shaw
10. Stevens

Alpha Filing, Rules 4-5

A. NAME	**PROPER INDEXING ORDER**
Edwina Suzanne Natrene	Natrene, Edwina Suzanne
Susan P. von Adams	Vonadams, Susan P
Marie Susan del Salva	delsalva, Marie Susan
Kellie Lucille O'Reilly	Oreilly, Kellie Lucille
Professor Simon Kalmbeck	Kalmbeck, Simon Professor
Lynn V. Utrect, M.D.	Utrett, Lynn V MD
Reverand Alvin de Laurent	deLaurent, Alvin Reverand
Edward Smith-Nelson	Smithnelson, Edward
Susan-Leigh Davis	Davis, Susanleigh
Robert Vincent MacCarty	Maccarty, Robert Vincent

B. PROPER ALPHABETIC ORDER

1. Davis
2. delaurent
3. delsalva
4. Kalmbeck
5. Mccarty
6. Natrene

7. Oreilly
8. Smithnelson
9. Utrect
10. Vonadams

Alpha Filing, Rules 6-7

A. NAME	PROPER INDEXING ORDER
Theodore Vincent Moore, III	Moore, Theodore Vincent III
Vincent T. Las Casos, Jr.	Lascasos, Vincent T Jr
Mrs. Shelly E. Truckson	Truckson, Shelly E Mrs
Franklin D. Wolchecki, II	Wolchecki, Franklin D II
Vincent T. Las Casos, Sr.	Lascasos, Vincent T Sr
Theodore Moore Vincent, Jr.	Vincent, Theodore Moore Jr
Franklin D. Wolchecki, IV	Wolchecki, Franklin D IV
Mrs. Herbert Grunlund (Sallie)	Grunlund, Herbert Mrs. (Sallie-X)
Vincent L. Las Casos, III	Lascasos, Vincent L III
Franklin D. Wollecki, Sr.	Wollecki, Franklin D Sr

B. PROPER ALPHABETIC ORDER

1. Grunlund
2. Lacasos, Vincent L III
3. Lacasos, Vincent T Jr
4. Lacasos, Vincent T Sr
5. Moore
6. Truckson
7. Vincent
8. Wolchecki, Franklin II
9. Wolchecki, Franklin IV
10. Wollecki, Sr

Alpha Filing, Business/Organizations

A. NAME	PROPER INDEXING ORDER AND CHARACTERS
Economy Billing Services	Economy Billing Services
Alpha & Omega Medical Supplies	Alpha and Omega Medical Supplies

The Friendly Taxi Service	Friendly Taxi Service The
23rd Street Hospital	23 Street Hospital
Bradley's Home Health Aides	Bradleys Home Health Aides
First Street Clinic	First Street Clinic
Speedy Transcription 4-U	Speedy Transcription 4U
The Quick-Fix Consultants	Quickfix Consultants The
Twenty-Second Answering Service	Twentysecond Answering Service
Mc-Adams Linen Supply	Mcadams Linen Supply
$20 Janitorial Service	20dollar Janitorial Service
WA Medical Supplies	WA Medical Supplies
Allenmoore Medical Center, 339 6th Avenue, Topeka, Kansas	Allenmore Medical Center Topeka Kansas 6 Avenue 339
Allenmoore Medical Center, 822 8th Avenue, Apple, Wisconsin	Allenmore Medical Center Apple Wisconsin 8 Avenue 822
Allenmoore Medical Center, 133 5th Avenue West, Topeka, Kansas	Allenmore Medical Center Topeka Kansas 5 Avenue West 133

B. PROPER ALPHABETIC ORDER

1. 20dollar
2. 23
3. Allenmoore, Apple
4. Allenmoore, Topeka, Kansas, 5
5. Allenmoore, Topeka, Kansas, 6
6. Alpha
7. Bradleys
8. Economy
9. First

10. Friendly
11. Mcadams
12. Quickfix
13. Speedy
14. Twentysecond
15. WA

****

NOTE: **In filing *medical charts*, the patient's *legal name* is always used. Rules 2, 3, and 6, listed below, therefore, apply to filing/labeling of materials other than patient charts such as with miscellaneous correspondence received in the office, employment applications, inquiries, magazines, private letters, etc. You will always obtain patients' legal names for their charts and index those rather than "as written."**

****

Individual Names

Rule 1: The names of individuals are assigned indexing units respectively: last name (surname), first name, middle name, and succeeding names.

Rule 2: If the item you are indexing uses an *initial* rather than a complete name, *index it as it is written.*

Rule 3: If the item you are indexing uses *abbreviations* or *nicknames* rather than a complete name, *index it as it is written.*

Rule 4: *Foreign language prefixes are indexed as one unit with the unit that follows. Spacing, punctuation and capitalization are ignored. Such prefixes include d, da, de, de la, del, des, di, du, el, fitz, l, la, las, le, les, lu, m, mac, mc, o, saint, sainte, san, santa, sao, st, te, ten, ter, van, van de, van der, and von der.* (*St, sainte, saint are *indexed as written*).

Rule 5: Titles are considered as separate indexing units. If the *title appears with first and last name, the title is considered to be the last indexing unit.*

Rule 6a: Names that are *hyphenated are considered as one unit.*

Rule 6b: When indexing the name of a *married woman,* the name is indexed *as used.* If the woman is known by her first name and her surname, these would be the indexing units. However, if the woman uses the title "Mrs.", her husband's first name, and then the surname, these would be the primary indexing units for filing purposes (see cross-referencing).

Rule 7a: *Seniority units* are indexed as the *last indexing unit.*

Rule 7b: *Seniorty units* are filed in *numerical order* from first to last.

Rule 7c: These numeric units are broken down such that *numeric seniority terms are filed before alphabetic terms.*

Businesses and Organizations

When indexing businesses and organizations, the rules you have learned under *individual names* will be used when individual names appear as part of the filing units (rules 1-7).

Rule 8: The *order* for indexing businesses/organizations is *as written.*

Rule 9: When "the" is the first unit of a business/organization, it is *indexed as the last unit.*

Rule 10a: *Symbols* are indexed as units and *spelled out as words.* Such symbols include &, ¢, $, #, and %.

Rule 10b: In indexing the "$" *sign before a number,* the *first unit is the number.*

Rule 11: When *punctuation marks* are included as part of the indexing units, they are *disregarded.* Punctuation marks include: . " ' : ; - ! ? ( ).

Rule 12a: When indexing *numbers,* the numbers are indexed as *written.*

Rule 12b: When indexing *figures,* the numbers are *written as figures and considered as one unit. Note:* d, nd, rd, st, and th are ignored when indexing.

Rule 12c: When *indexing numbers,* if the number is written as a single word it *is indexed as a single unit.*

Rule 12d: When *indexing numbers,* if the number is *written with a word,* it is *indexed as one unit with the word and filed in ascending order before alphabetic names.*

Rule 12e: When indexing *hyphenated numbers,* they are indexed *only by the number before the hyphen.*

Rule 12f: When indexing *alpha characters and numeric characters,* the numeric characters are always filed *before alpha characters.*

Rule 13: When indexing words which can be *compound or two single words,* the "as written" rule applies. (Consider whether it is appropriate to cross-reference hyphenated words.)

Rule 14: When *names of business/clinics,* etc. are *identical,* the *address may be used for ordering of the files.* The address is indexed by:
CITY → STATE → STREET NAME → ADDRESS #

APPENDIX

B

Tab Alpha Labels
Alpha-Z Labels
Variadex Labels
Color-Coded Labels
Subject Labels
Geographic Labels
Alphabetic & Blank Labels

In this appendix you will find sticky-back labels for the filing projects. Following are legends for the color-coded labels. You will need to color-code the label letters before applying the labels to the charts. If you do not have these colors available, design a legend for the colors you will be using for the labels. Also provided are blank labels to be used for the correspondence-filing assignments as well as the subject and geographic labels.

Tab Alpha Legend

A	Red	M	Lt Green
B	Lt Orange	N	Dk Green
C	Dk Orange	O	Blue
D	Lt Green	P	Violet
E	Dk Green	Q	Lavender
F	Blue	R	Brown
G	Violet	S	Pink
H	Lavender	T	Red
I	Pink	U	Lt Orange
J	Red	V	Dk Orange
K	Lt Orange	W	Dk Green
L	Dk Orange	X	Blue
Mc	Brown	Y	Violet
		Z	Lavender

Tab Alpha Labels, #1

A A A A A A A A

A A B B B B B B

B B D D D D D D

D D E E E E E E

E E E E E E E E

E E G G G G G G

G G H H H H H H

H H H H I I I I

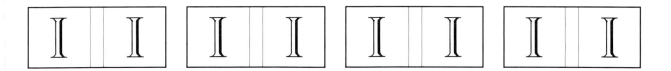

Each label contains two letters with a bar for color-coding in between.

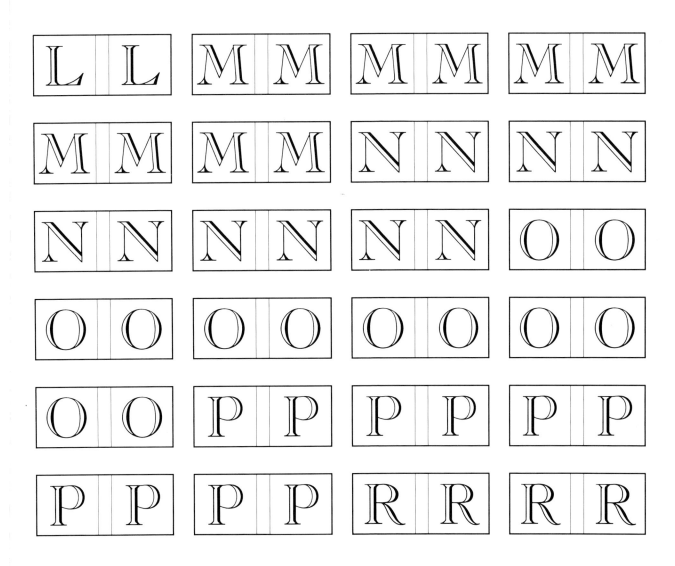

Permanent

U.S. Patent #4,790,805

FasTrack™

U.S. Patent #4,790,805

FasTrack™

Permanent

Permanent

U.S. Patent #4,790,805

FasTrack™

Permanent

U.S. Patent #4,790,805

FasTrack™

U.S. Patent #4,790,805

FasTrack™

Permanent

Permanent

U.S. Patent #4,790,805

FasTrack™

Permanent

U.S. Patent #4,790,805

FasTrack™

U.S. Patent #4,790,805

FasTrack™

Permanent

Permanent

U.S. Patent #4,790,805

FasTrack™

Permanent

U.S. Patent #4,790,805

FasTrack™

U.S. Patent #4,790,805

FasTrack™

R R R R R R R R

S S S S S S S S

S S S S S S S S

T T T T T T T T

T T T T U U U U

U U U U U U

ALPHA-Z LEGEND

(A-M—White Letter, Color Background)
(N-Z—Color Letter, White Background)

A, N	Red
B, O	Dark Blue
C, P	Dark Green
D, Q	Light Blue
E, R	Purple
F, S	Orange
G, T	Gray
H, U	Dark Brown
I, V	Pink
J, W	Yellow
K, X	Light Brown
L, Y	Lavender
M, Z	Light Green

Alpha-Z Labels, #1

FasTrack™

Permanent

U.S. Patent #4,790,805

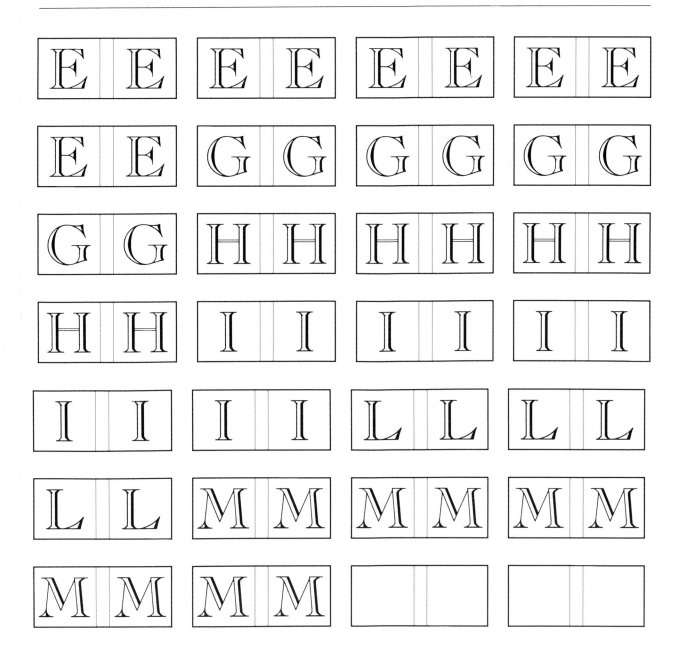

A label contains two letters with a bar in between.

Alpha-Z Labels, #1 (Cont'd)

Permanent

Permanent

U.S. Patent #4,790,805

FasTrack™

Permanent

U.S. Patent #4,790,805

FasTrack™

U.S. Patent #4,790,805

FasTrack™

Permanent

Permanent

U.S. Patent #4,790,805

FasTrack™

Permanent

U.S. Patent #4,790,805

FasTrack™

U.S. Patent #4,790,805

FasTrack™

Permanent

Permanent

U.S. Patent #4,790,805

FasTrack™

Permanent

U.S. Patent #4,790,805

FasTrack™

U.S. Patent #4,790,805

FasTrack™

Permanent

Permanent

U.S. Patent #4,790,805

FasTrack™

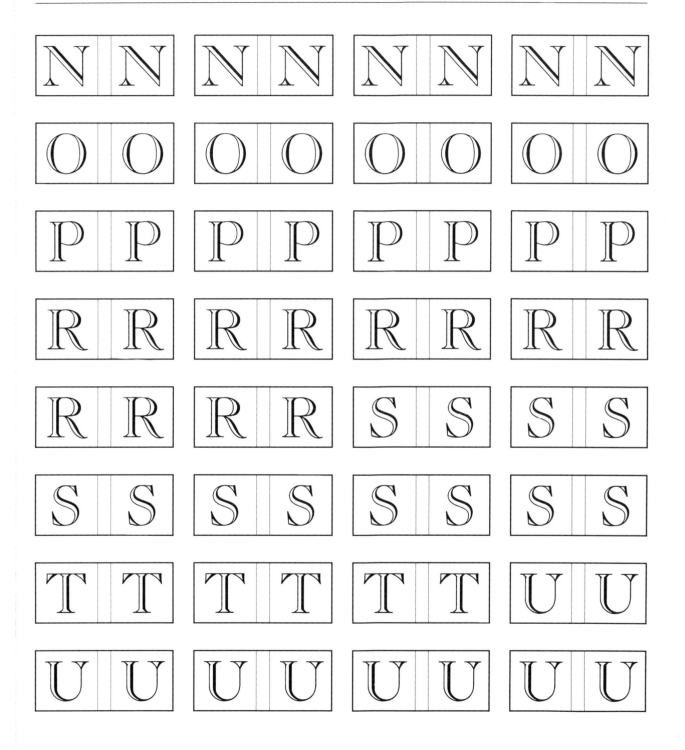

FasTrack™

Permanent

U.S. Patent #4,790,805

Variadex

(2nd letter coded)

a, b, c, d	Orange
e, f, g, h	Yellow
i, j, k, l, m, n	Green
o, p, q	Blue
r, st, t, u, v, w,	
x, y, z	Violet

Variadex Labels

ORANGE	ORANGE	ORANGE
ORANGE	ORANGE	ORANGE
ORANGE	ORANGE	ORANGE
ORANGE	ORANGE	ORANGE
ORANGE	ORANGE	ORANGE
YELLOW	YELLOW	YELLOW
YELLOW	YELLOW	YELLOW

You are to use the proper colored label and type the patient's name below.

GREEN

BLACK, Charles P.

Variadex Labels

BLUE	BLUE	BLUE
BLUE	BLUE	BLUE
BLUE	BLUE	BLUE
BLUE	BLUE	BLUE
VIOLET	VIOLET	VIOLET
VIOLET	VIOLET	VIOLET
GREEN	GREEN	GREEN
GREEN	GREEN	GREEN
GREEN	GREEN	GREEN
GREEN	GREEN	GREEN
GREEN	GREEN	GREEN
BLUE	BLUE	BLUE

Color-Coded Numbers

0	0	0	0	0	0	0	0	0
1	1	1	2	2	2	2	2	2
2	2	2	2	3	3	3	3	3
3	3	3	4	4	4	4	4	4
5	5	5	5	6	6	6	6	6
7	7	7	7	7	7	7	7	8
8	8	8	8	8	8	8	8	8
8	8	9	9	9	9	9	9	9
9	9	9	9	0	1	2	3	4
5	6	7	8	9	0	1	2	3

Color-Code Legend

0	Brown	5	Yellow
1	Blue	6	Red
2	Teal	7	Dk Orange
3	Lt Orange	8	Violet
4	Green	9	Pink

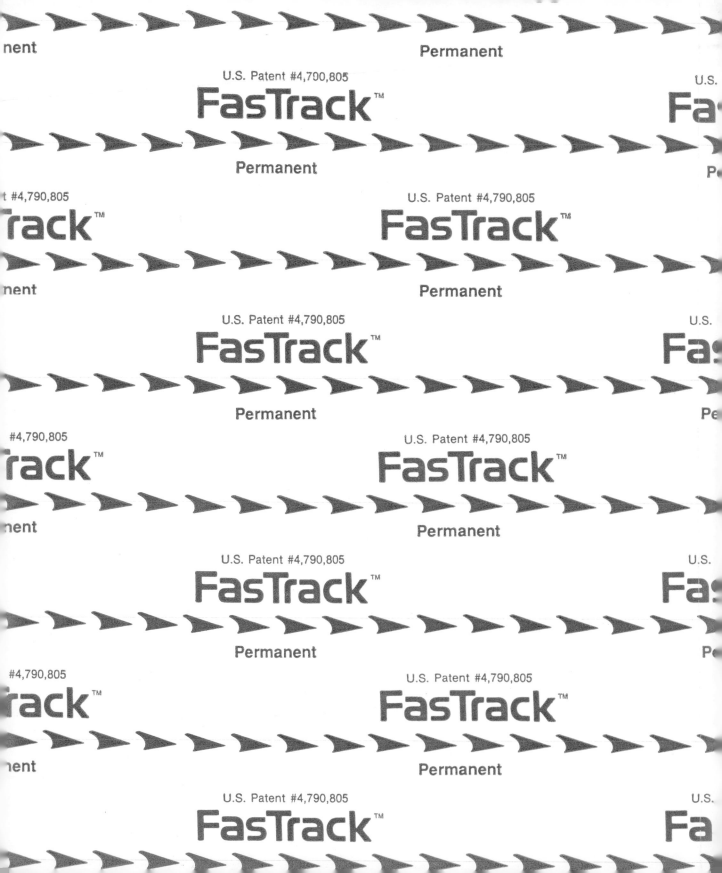

Subject Labels

PHARMACIES
DRUG CO/REPS
HOME HEALTH
MEDICAL EQUIPMENT
OFFICE SUPPLIES
HOSPITALS

Geographic Labels

NEW YORK-A	MONTANA-A
MICHIGAN-A	WASH-A
FLORIDA-A	TEXAS-A
CALIF-A	NEW JERSEY-A
OKLA-A	MASS-A
KENTUCKY-A	PENN-A
ARIZONA-A	OREGON-A

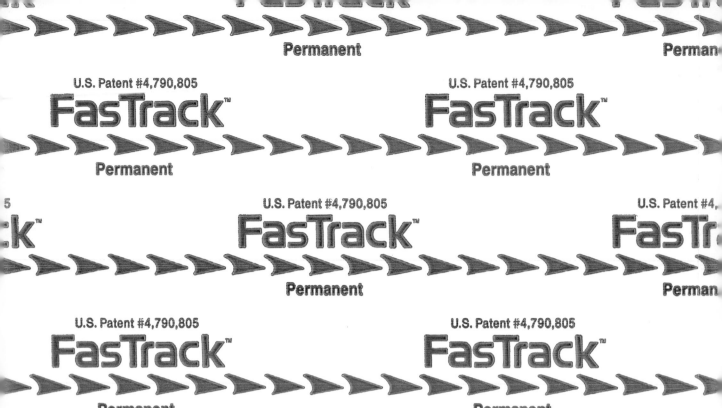

IDAHO-A	VIRGINIA-A
MISSOURI-A	OREGON-B
WASH-B	IDAHO-B
Albany-A	*Cortland-A*
Kalispell-A	*Lansing-A*
Shelby-A	*Spokane-A*
Tacoma-A	*Ann Arbor-A*
Miami-A	*Bellingham-A*
Houston-A	*Los Angeles-A*
Lakewood-A	Tulsa-A
Boston-A	Louisville-A
Pittsburgh-A	Tucson-A
Salem-A	Austin-A
Boise-A	Paradise Valley-A
Kimball-A	Aberdeen-A

Permanent

FasTrack™

U.S. Patent #4,790,805

Permanent

FasTrack™

U.S. Patent #4,790,805

Permanent

FasTrack™

U.S. Patent #4,790,805

Permanent

FasTrack™

U.S. Patent #4,790,805

Permanent

FasTrack™

U.S. Patent #4,790,805

Permanent

FasTrack™

U.S. Patent #4,790,805

Permanent

FasTrack™

U.S. Patent #4,790,805

Permanent

FasTrack™

U.S. Patent #4,790,805

Permanent

FasTrack™

U.S. Patent #4,790,805

Permanent

FasTrack™

U.S. Patent #4,790,805

Pocatello-A	Springfield-A
Shawnee-A	Bluefield-A
Amarillo-A	Medford-A
Pocatello-B	Othello-B
Shelby-B	Spokane-B
Medford-B	Bellingham-B
Federal Way-B	Boise-B
Twin Falls-B	Portland-B
Klam. Falls-B	Seattle-B
Richland-B	Hermiston-B
Everett-B	Yakima-B
Canyon Riv-B	Port Angeles-B
Forks-B	Newport-B
Salem-B	Pocatello-B

FasTrack™

U.S. Patent #4,790,805

Permanent

Idaho Falls-B	Grangeville-B
Ketchum-B	Spokane-B
Westport-B	LaGrande-B
Salmon-B	Orofino-B
Blaine-B	

Alphabetic and Blank Labels, #1

A	B	C	D
E	F	G	H
I	J	K	L
M	N	O	P
Q	R	S	T
U	V	W	X
Y	Z		

APPENDIX

C

Materials for Filing Projects

Cards for Assignment 1

1. Edward L. Tucker
2. Donald B. Fingarson
3. Alvin Lee Kowalsky
4. Richard C. Andersen
5. Jean Nadine Higdon
6. Kenneth Daniel Beckman
7. David T. Ames
8. Domingo P. Ceralde
9. Frederick Hershel Montgomery
10. Bobbie Louise Allison
11. Ellen Michelle Epstein
12. Patrick Grady Rose
13. David Merin Grellier
14. James L. Caruthers
15. Charles Christopher Inge
16. Brian Adam Bouton
17. Ronald Craig Roberts
18. Tony Neil Uhinck
19. Lois C. Beswick
20. Herbert Calvin Abbs

Cards for Assignment 2

21. Professor Harold Hill
22. Susan Alexandra O'Malley
23. Albert Michael Ashlock, III
24. Thomas P. Diamond-Wells
25. Allison-Sue Jolene Richmond
26. Capt. Irin Lionel Atridge
27. William Christopher McAdams
28. Kenneth Steven Trenary-Hill
29. Alfred James Vannyson
30. JoAnn Nadine Saint Claire
31. Rose-Marie Susan Ticehurst
32. Dr. Richard P. Collins
33. Mrs. Lawrence J. Trigg
34. Michael Ryan Tichurst
35. Shawn Paul MacPherson
36. Katsuko Margine Workman
37. James Frye van der Vorn
38. Judith Defora Triggs
39. Albert Michael Ashlock, Jr.
40. Carl Roger St. Simons

Cards for Assignment 3

41. Yamamoto Medical Supplies
42. Professional Nursing Service
43. Allard's Outpatient Clinic
44. The Surgical Supply Wearhouse
45. Farrell's Home Health
46. O'Donnell's Orthotic Supplies
47. McKinney-McGrath Plastic Surgeons
48. Leonhart & Browning Bookkeeping
49. The Visual Connection
50. Bronson-Metlinson Physical Therapy
51. Hedahl's Home Health Service
52. Boise Convalescent & Rehabilitation Center
53. The Ridgetop Convalescent Center
54. Your Doctor's Telephone Message Service
55. Allenmore-Billings Medical Center
56. The Superior Janitorial Service
57. Superior Nursing Home
58. Treuax Transcription Service
59. A Personal Choice Birthing Center
60. Ron's Linen Service

Cards for Assignment 4

61. Flowers-to-Go, Aberdeen
62. West Sound Physical Therapy
63. 68th Street Doctors Clinic
64. Doc Brownley's Nutritional Supplies
65. Helen's Home Health, 76 Tweed, Biloxi, Missouri
66. South West Physical Therapy
67. Flowers To Go, Puyallup
68. Thirty-Third Avenue Quality Care
69. Westsound Medical Supplies
70. Helen's Home Health, 91 Tukwila, Biloxi, Missouri
71. Ellen's Handy Helpers Temporary Office Help
72. Liske Treatment Center
73. 2 No Avail Tax Accounting
74. Jefferson Home Health, 5891 10th Avenue, Chicken, Alabama
75. Southeast Referral Service
76. Access 2-U Medical Supplies
77. Liske's Plastic Surgery Center
78. The Temporary Aides
79. Jefferson Home Health, 5791 10th Avenue, Port Arthur, Texas
80. Bradley-Morton Memorial Hospital

Cards for Assignment 5

81. Long Trong Weesong
82. Claudette Jean Taylor-Young
83. Marks-Spateman & Realto, Surgeons
84. Christeen E. Morgan-Downs (Mrs. Lawrence)
85. Mrs. Timothy Uhler (Dawn)
86. Zacher, Prichard and Long, Attorneys
87. Teang Sing Luao
88. Daniel William Rose-Nelson
89. Gruber-Swartz & Associates
90. Geane Kathleen Moore (Mrs. David)

Assignment 6: Filing Procedures, #1

PHYSICIAN ORDERS

PATIENT:

duChesneu, Myrtle

#	ORDER DATE	CODE	ORDER TEXT
1	11/12/91	01	Diet: 200 ADA w/reg texture
2	11/14/91	02	Allow pt on dietary restrictions to partake of special meals 1 × month—texture as ordered.
3	6/18/92	T1	Diascan 2 days/wk AC bkfst/dinner—call MD if above 250-clarification of order
4	10/12/92	M	Ferrous sulfate 5 gr po bid

PHYSICIAN NAME   PHONE

MCLEAN, Oscar   341-9982

Assignment 6: Filing Procedures, #2

1

2

3

4

5
IN THE SUPERIOR COURT OF THE STATE OF WASHINGTON
IN AND FOR THE COUNTY OF CLALLAM

6 DREWKOWSKY, Andrew, a single
man
      Plaintiff,   )   No. 89-2-015276

7 v.

8 Swanson Brothers Construction,
      et al.,

9   Defendants.

)
)
)
)
)
)
)
)
)
)
)
)
)
)

STIPULATION RE
AND AUTHORIZATION
FOR HEALTH CARE
RECORDS OF
  ANDREW DREWKOWSKY

SSN: 374-02-0998
DOB: 8/16/43

10 The parties hereto stipulate and agree as follows:

11 A. To facilitate orderly discovery in this matter, the defendant may obtain copies of all medical records regarding Andrew Drewkowski from the following health care provider:

12

(1) Thomas P. Sheridan, M.D.
3306 Harbell Drive SW
Halloway, OR 97403

13

Assignment 6: Filing Procedures, #3

AUTHORIZATION TO RELEASE
PATIENT MEDICAL INFORMATION

PATIENT NAME McLean, Oscar R.   CSR# 768628

FORMER NAME (if any) _____   BIRTHDATE 4/14/34

INFORMATION TO BE RELEASED: RELEASE TO:

ORGANIZATION Thomas P. Sheridan, M.D.   NAME Northwest Rehab

ADDRESS 3306 Harbell Drive SW   ADDRESS 833 Ecklund

Halloway, OR 97403   Eastside, OR 97405

PHONE (503) 282-0032   PHONE (503) 397-4508

PURPOSE OR NEED FOR THIS INFORMATION IS: Carpal tunnel exam

I hereby authorize Thomas P. Sheridan _____ to release the following medical information

concerning myself/ Oscar R. McLean   :

TYPE OF RECORD   DATES OF TREATMENT

___X___ ALL medical records   FROM 8/13/91 TO 9/14/92

_____ CLINIC records only

_____ HOSPITAL records only

_____ COMMUNITY HEALTH records only

_____ LAB RESULTS (specify) _____

_____ X-RAY REPORT/FILM (specify) _____

_____ OTHER RECORDS (specify) _____

**Records containing information relating to drug, alcohol, mental health, and sexually transmitted disease testing, diagnosis, and treatment require a SPECIAL AUTHORIZATION.

I hereby authorize _____NA_____ to release the following PROTECTED medical information

concerning myself/ Oscar R. McLean   :

_____ Drug abuse diagnosis/treatment   FROM _____ TO _____

_____ Alcoholism diagnosis/treatment

_____ Mental health diagnosis/treatment

_____ Sexually transmitted disease
diagnosis/treatment or counseling

Assignment 6, Filing Procedures, #4

LABORATORY REPORT

PATIENT: NORTON, Daphne Lynn   AGE: 14   SEX: F   DATE: 8/06/92

LABORATORY REPORT #: 20834100-A

WBC	RBC	HGB	HCT	PLATELETS	ESR	RETICS	POLYS	BANDS	LYMPHS	MONOS	EOS	BASO	

COLOR	APPEAR	SP GRAVITY	PH	PROT	GLUC	KET	OCC BLOOD	CASTS	CRYSTALS	BACT

GLUCOSE	BUN	CREAT	URIC AC	PHOS	CALCIUM	TOT PROT	ALBUMIN	TOTAL BILI

PAGE 1 OF 1   ----LAST PAGE----

DILANTIN   26.6   10--20   MCG/ML ..H

LAST DOSE 8.5 HR AGO

RESULTS THOMAS P. SHERIDAN, M.D.

ORDERED BY: HARRIET T. WONG, M.D.

CHART RPT 08/04/92 18:25

Assignment 6, Filing Procedures, #5

AUTHORIZATION FOR PATIENT SERVICES

SERIAL NO.	START DATE	EXP. DATE	REFERRED BY
#367900	6/25/92	7/25/92	Allen B. Henson, M.D.

PATIENT:
Mrs. Herbert E. Downs (Sarah)

REFERRED TO:
Thomas P. Sheridan, M.D.
3306 Harbell Drive SW
Halloway, OR 97403
(503) 282-0032
SPECIALTY: Orthopedics

TYPE
Outpatient

URGENCY
Routine

ATTENDING PRACTIONER

SERVICES/PROCEDURES/GOODS REQUESTED

Provide one consultation/second opinion only

QTY	CODE	DESCRIPTION
One	90050	Limited visit established patient

DESCRIPTION
Followup exam

SEE REVERSE SIDE FOR IMPORTANT INSTRUCTIONS

COVERED CONTRACT #   C00268
CONTRACT TYPE: Group
DEDUCTIBLE $50

IF YOU HAVE QUESTIONS REGARDING THIS REFERRAL, PLEASE CONTACT:

Valley Springs Medical Clinic
78009 Wetlands Boulevard
Treasury, OR 97509
(503) 683-0777

LAB AND RADIOLOGY SERVICES MUST BE PERFORMED AT VALLEY SPRINGS MEDICAL CLINIC.

Assignment 6: Filing Procedures, #6

EXPERT IMAGING INC.

4039 Sylvan Way   Bremerton, WA (206)476-3209

Patient's Name: CUERTO, Augustus   Age: 34

Today's Date: 11/12/92

Referring Physician: Thomas P. Sheridan, M.D.

CLINICAL INFORMATION: Recent onset of seizures and blurred
vision.

EXAM PERFORMED: COMPUTED TOMOGRAPHY OF THE HEAD

A computed tomographic study of the head is conducted utilizing transaxial images at 10-mm increments from base to vertex. No midline displacement is observed. The ventricular system is modestly prominent. No extra-axial fluid is identified and no localized areas of altered attenuation are seen within the cerebral substance.

With injection of contrast material intravenously, no areas of abnormal augmentation are identifed. No extra-axial fluid is seen. Osseous structures about the base of the brain are within normal limits.

CONCLUSION: CT examination of the head shows mild atrophy. No evidence of intracranial space-occupying lesion.

Elaine O. Mossman

ELAINE O. MOSSMAN, M.D./klk

D: 11/12/92
T: 11/14/92

Assignment 6: Filing Procedures, #7

AUTHORIZATION FOR MEDICAL INFORMATION

This authorization, or photocopy hereof, will authorize you to furnish:

___✓___ Northwest Insurance Co.   _____ State Employees Mutual

all information you may have regarding my condition while under your observa-
tion or treatment, including the history obtained. X-rays, physical findings,
diagnosis and prognosis.

Bartrum Rigelson   *March 15, 1992*
_____
       Signature   Date

AUTHORIZATION FOR WAGE AND SALARY INFORMATION

This authorization, or photocopy hereof, will authorize you to furnish:

___✓___ Northwest Insurance Co.   _____ State Employees Mutual

all information you may have regarding my wages or salary while employed by
you.

Bartrum Rigelson   *March 15, 1992*
_____
       Signature   Date

Social Security Number _____

Assignment 6: Filing Procedures, #8

EXPERT IMAGING INC.

4039 Sylvan Way   Bremerton, WA (206)476-3209

Patient's Name: Saint James, Keith W.   Age: 56

Today's Date: 9/16/91

Referring Physician: Thomas P. Sheridan, M.D.

CLINICAL INFORMATION: SP MVA in 8/91 with low-back pain × six months. Pain and numbness in right leg greater than left leg.

EXAM PERFORMED: COMPUTED TOMOGRAPHY OF THE LUMBAR SPINE

TECHNIQUE: Nonenhanced computed tomography of the lumbosacral spine was performed using 3 to 5-mm contiguous axial sections angled through the L3-4 through L5-S1 intervertebral disc spaces.

INTERPRETATION: L3-4 intervertebral discs demonstrate normal disc density and contour. The neural foramen and facet joints bilaterally are normal.

The L4-5 intervertebral discs demonstrate normal disc density. However, there is a broad-based asymmetrical focal contour abnormality measuring approximately 5 mm in AP dimension that indents the ventral surface of the thecal sac and narrows the subarticular recesses bilaterally. The imaging findings suggest impingement upon the traversing L5 nerve roots bilaterally. Imaging findings are consistent with a large disc protrusion versus extrusion.

IMPRESSION: Moderate-sized broad-based disc protrusion at the L4-5 level which narrows the subarticular recesses bilaterally suggesting impingement upon the traversing L5 nerve roots bilaterally.

Benjamin E. Renton

BENJAMIN E. RENTON, M.D.

D: 9/16/91
T: 9/17/91

Assignment 6: Filing Procedures, #9

THOMAS P. SHERIDAN, M.D.
3306 Harbell Drive SW
Halloway, OR 97403
(503) 282-0032

PHYSICAL ACTIVITY REQUIREMENTS

Patient: FORRESTER, Lance   Age: 28

C = constantly, F = frequently, O = occasionally, S = Seldom, N = Never

A. Lifting:
1-10 lbs	F
11-24 lbs	S
25-50 lbs	S
over 50 lbs	N

B: Carrying:
1-10 lbs	S
11-24 lbs	S
25-50 lbs	S
over 50 lbs	N

C. Pushing/Pulling:
1-10 lbs	F
11-24 lbs	S
25-50 lbs	N
over 50 lbs	N

D. Reaching:
above shoulder	S
at shoulder hgt	F
below shoulder	F
grasping	F

ADDITIONAL COMMENTS: The only moderately heavy item handled would be carpet cleaning equipment, maximum 11-24 lbs, main equipment on wheels. Assistance is available for a lifting involved with position.

Thomas P. Sheridan M.D.

THOMAS P. SHERIDAN, M.D.

Assignment 6: Filing Procedures, #10

1

2

3   BEFORE THE BOARD OF INDUSTRIAL INSURANCE APPEALS

4   STATE OF WASHINGTON

5   IN RE THE CLAIM OF

6   Eugenia Louise Williams   )   DOCKET NO. 03-2698-3266
)
7   )   NOTICE OF DEPOSITION
)   UPON ORAL EXAMINATION
8   CLAIM NO. J4982092   )   IN LIEU OF TESTIMONY
    _____)
9   TO: Alex Cubek, Industrial Insurance Appeals Judge;
    AND TO: Simon N. Farstead, Assistant Attorney General,
10 Office of the Attorney General
    AND TO: Thomas P. Sheridan, M.D.
11
    YOU, AND EACH OF YOU, WILL PLEASE TAKE NOTICE, that
12 testimony of Thomas P. Sheridan, M.D., will be taken by
    oral examination at the instistence and request of the
13 claimant in the above-entitled action, before a notary
    public at the office of Thomas P. Sheridan—
14
    on Monday, November 25, 1989, commencing at the
15 hour of 2:00 p.m., the said oral examination to be
    subject to continuance or adjournment from time to
16 time or place to place until completed.

17 DATED: October 3, 1989

Assignment 7: Color-Coding

David Barrett II, #826092

John-Phillippe Douglas, Tab-Alpha

Michael V. Swanson, Tab-Alpha

Capt. Murray T. Leskowsky, Alpha-Z

Hollister McKenzie, Sr., #380204

Edward Anthony Mac Call, Alpha-Z

Margaret Hilton-Babniuk, Tab-Alpha

Sylvester Medical Supplies, Variadex

South-Side Ambulance Service, #77829

A-1 Medical Supplies, Alpha-Z

Sara DiGeorge, Tab-Alpha

South-Side Ambulance Service, #77829

A-1 Medical Supplies, Alpha-Z

Sara DiGeorge, Tab-Alpha

Rosanne Montgomery, Variadex

Dana Pauline Middleton, #380004

Mrs. Rosa Tenney, Tab-Alpha

Mrs. Manuel Tenney (Maria), Alpha-Z

Steven B. Innes, Tab-Alpha

Vincent M. LeClare, #78728

Ninth Street Emergency Clinic, Variadex

Druscilla E. Grimes, Alpha-Z

Robert W. Thorsen, Variadex

Noah W. Cole-Porter, #68402

Bruce E. Baird, Variadex

Denise E. del Satas, Tab-Alpha

Shur-Fit Optical, Alpha-Z

Ms. Ellen T. Sanders, #39039

Sarah Dupont, Tab-Alpha

Samuel Earl Wilkens, Variadex

Alexander Olson Grimes, Alpha-Z

Donald J. Finn, #866092

Rosanne Louise Murphy, Tab-Alpha

Charles Edward Vicars, Variadex

Robert William Morris, Variadex

Assignment 8: Numeric Filing

Jackie Brigham, #570 16 3908

Richard Brady, #109 11 9083

Donna LaQuestran, #131 22 8306

Robert Frestrand, #083 14 9609

Barbara Medling, #083 16 3208

June Yescovich, #109 22 9609

Adelaide Humphrey, #131 16 3098

Charles Novak, #500 21 8761

Mary Ann Mosby, #572 11 6908

Stan Doxen, #5784 83 4942

Assignment 10: Subject Filing

#1   Bovine's Medical Supplies
1197 Pershing Court
Knoxville, TN

#2   Keizer Memorial Hospital
200 Fairway Drive
Newport, OR

#3   Hyrex Pharmaceuticals
270 NE Watson Court
Newark, NJ

#4   Tri-County Business Equipment
380 Sidney Avenue
Caldwell, OR

#5   Baker's Day and Night Drugs
6842 Farwest Drive
Simpson, OR

#6   Hyrex Pharmaceuticals
245 Alamaine Lane
Boston, MA

#7   Gerald P. Slezak
Maltbie Pharmaceuticals
PO Box 9426
Ferndale, NY

#8   Home Hospital Needs
1260 NW Huckle Drive
Clindon, OR

Assignment 10: Subject Filing (Cont'd)

#9   The Professional Office
      4418 Olympus Drive NE
      Pleasanton, OR

#10   Monsanto Chemical Company
      542 Silver Creek Road
      Faraway, OR

#11   McLendon Quick Prescriptions
      4009 West County Road
      Austin, OR

#12   Peltzer County Hospital
      4884 Lakeview Boulevard
      Little Park, OR

#13   La Salle Surgical Company
      4995 Alpenglow Drive NW
      Portland, OR

#14   Skaggs Business Organizers
      1328 Morgan Road East
      Tiara, OR

#15   Cheryl Flodin
      Daywell Laboratories
      PO Box 317
      Butler, NJ

#16   Farrell's Health Equipment
      7429 Pioneer Lane SW
      Little Park, OR

#17   Fiedler's Drug Emporium
      9493 Towne Road
      Misery, OR

#18   Jackson Park Hospital
      1307 NW Mirage Lane
      Wholesome, OR

#19   Dermik Laboratories
      700 North Sepulveda Boulevard
      Copiague, NY

#20   Roth's Rental Supplies
      4868 NW Eldorado Court
      McAllister, OR

#21   Emerson Surgical Suppliers
        2680 SE Kari Court
        Allenton, PA

#22   Flint Laboratories
        1425 Lake Shore Drive
        Northridge, CA

#24   Tri-County Business Equipment
        1910 Ninth Avenue South
        Portland, OR

#25   Wilder Laboratories
        1932 Pioneer Road
        Whitsorth, VT

Assignment 11: Geographic Filing

#1   Alex Flores, Male, Age 43
Born: Albany, NY
Raised: Age 1-7   Ithica, NY
            Age 8-10   Newark, NJ

#2   David Landerman, Male, Age 28
Born: Cortland, NY
Raised: Age 1-3   Miami, FL
            Age 4-8   Newark, NJ
            Age 9-10   Brooklyn, NY

#3   James Straderm, Male, Age 24
Born: Kalispell, MT
Raised: Age 1-10   Pocatello, ID

#4   Roberta Linde, Female, Age 34
Born: Lansing, MI
Raised: Age 1-6   Othello, WA
            Age 7-10   Prairie Plains, OR

#5   Rickey Vinson, Male, Age 53
Born: Shelby, WA
Raised: Age 1-8   Shelby, WA
            Age 9-10   Medford, OR

#6   Anthony Floreske, Male, Age 32
Born: Spokane, WA
Raised: Age 1-10   Spokane, WA

Assignment 11: Geographic Filing (Cont'd)

#7   Evan Margrave, Male, Age 44
Born: Tacoma, WA
Raised: Age 1-4   Bellingham, WA
           Age 5-8   Federal Way, WA
           Age 9-10   Pittsburg, PA

#8   William Olsen, Male, Age 37
Born: Ann Arbor, MI
Raised: Age 1-3   Lansing, MI
           Age 4-6   Boise, ID
           Age 7-10   Twin Falls, ID

#9   Jessica Kao, Female, Age 26
Born: Miami, FL
Raised: Age 1-7   Portland, OR
           Age 8-10   Miami, FL

#10   Denise Romnes, Female, Age 22
Born: Bellingham, WA
Raised: Age 1-3   Blaine, WA
           Age 4-10   Mesa, AZ

#11   Janine Lutz, Female, Age 36
Born: Houston, TX
Raised: Age 1-2   Los Angeles, CA
           Age 3-10   Klamath Falls, OR

#12   Larry Williams, Male, Age 24
Born: Los Angeles, CA
Raised: Age 1-4   Bakersfield, CA
           Age 5-7   Portland, OR
           Age 8-10   Seattle, WA

#13   Ninette Thompson, Female, Age 38
Born: Winaschotia, NH
Raised: Age 1-5   Granite Falls, NH
           Age 6-8   Richland, WA
           Age 9-10   Portland, OR

#14   Shelby Resop, Female, Age 27
Born: Tulsa, OK
Raised: Age 1-9   Hermiston, OR
           Age 10   Oklahoma City, OK

#15   Oscar Riksheim, Male, Age 56
Born: Boston, MA
Raised: Age 1-10   Concrete, WA

Assignment 11: Geographic Filing (Cont'd)

#16 Kimberly Swan, Female, Age 22
Born: Louisville, KY
Raised: Age 1-7

#17 Cynthia Bruchaster, Female, Age 40
Born: Pittsburgh, PA
Raised: Age 1-2   Pittsburgh, PA
          Age 3-9   Port Angeles, WA
          Age 10   Forks, WA

#18 Don Swansboro, Male, Age 30
Born: Tucson, AZ
Raised: Age 1-9   Hermiston, OR
          Age 10   Tuscon, AZ

#19 Cathe Suzuki, Female, Age 28
Born: Salem, OR
Raised: Age 1-3   Portland, OR
          Age 4-10   Newport, OR

#20 David Unieski, Male, Age 32
Born: Austin, TX
Raised: Age 1-5   Klamath, OR
          Age 6-8   Dallas, TX
          Age 9-10   Salem, OR

#21 Sonja Yeager, Female, Age 28
Born: Boise, ID
Raised: Age 1-8   Pocatello, ID
          Age 9-10   Idaho, Falls, ID

#22 Joyce Ruddick, Female, Age 28
Born: Paradise Valley, CA
Raised: Age 1-7   Spokane, WA
          Age 8-10   Sacramento, CA

#23 Dale Holloway, Male, Age 36
Born: Kimball, VA
Raised: Age 1-7   Grangeville, ID
          Age 8-10   Ketchum, ID

#24 Micahela Peelman, Female, Age 29
Born: Aberdeen, WA
Raised: Age 1-10   Westport, WA

#25 Thomas Olanie, Male, Age 23
Born: Pocatello, ID
Raised: Age 1-3   Orofino, ID
          Age 4-10   Kingston, NC

Assignment 11: Geographic Filing (Cont'd)

#26   Andrew Peterson, Male, Age 42
Born: Springfield, MO
Raised: Age 1-2   Rolla, MO
           Age 3-5   Scotts Butte, OR
           Age 6-10   La Grande, OR

#27   Vivian Shafer, female, Age 34
Born: Shawnee, OK
Raised: Age 1-9   Salmon, ID
           Age 10   Stilwater, OK

#28   Mary Alice Quilacio, Female, Age 22
Born: Bluefield, VA
Raised: Age 1-2   Morgantown, VA
           Age 3-10   Twin Falls, ID

#29   Lorraine Matson, Female, Age 43
Born: Amarillo, TX
Raised: Age 1-3   Durant, OK
           Age 4-6   Coos Bay, OR
           Age 6-10   Salem, OR

#30   Philip Charness, Male, Age 27
Born: Medford, OR
Raised: Age 1-7   Grants Pass, OR
           Age 8-9   Redding, CA
           Age 9-10   Sacramento, CA

Assignment 12: Correspondence Filing, #1

ALLYN PHYSICAL THERAPY INC., P.S.
4308 Highway 14
Allyn, WA 97326
(503)465-1293

Mike Reacher, RPT   **Colleen Sanders, RPT**

Patient's name <u>Pauline DelSantos</u>   Date <u>6-12-90</u>

Total number of treatments <u>25</u> Total time <u>3 months</u>

Diagnosis <u>Disc Degeneration</u>

General results:

____ Pt's symptoms are absent

<u>XX</u> Pt's symptoms have decreased but continue

____ Pt's symptoms remain unchanged.

____ Pt's symptoms have increased.

Treatment: Ultrasound, hot packs, massage and pelvic traction. Patient started traction at 45# and increased traction to 70#.

Progress: Patient reported a good general decrease in all symptoms. Now low-back and left-hip pain is only produced by prolonged sitting. Patient has increased activities without increasing pain. Ambulation is now easier and the tenderness over left sciatic notch is decreasing also. Patient completed only two of the last six weeks of treatment prescribed and did not show for subsequent appointments.

Patient discharged from physical therapy.

Thank you for this referral.

Copy sent to <u>Doctor Sheridan</u>

<u>*Mike Reacher*</u>, RPT

Assignment 12: Correspondence Filing, #2

NAME Last	First	Middle I	Exam Date
Eckvinar, Colleen L			6/04/92

ADDRESS		AGE	DOB
3566 Helena Drive SE		40	8/16/40

CITY & STATE	ZIP CODE
Silverdale, WA	98383

HEALTHCHECK

MEDEXAM HEALTHCHECK is an economical health screening program designed to help establish priorities in medical treatment, help extend health care to those not receiving it, help identify disease at earlier stages.

NOTE: There are no copies of this evaluation. It was made for your personal use and/or consultation with your physician. Keep it with your other important papers for comparison with future evaluations, to use for insurance history, when hospitalized, etc.

> I hereby voluntarily consent to having a screening examination that will include a routine physical examination with blood tests. I also consent to having my blood pressure taken and recorded as part of the screening examination. I understand that no major risks are connected with this screening procedure and hereby release all **MEDEXAM** personnel from any liability related to the normal conduct of the screening process.

Date 6/04/92   Signature *Colleen L. Eckvinar*

IF YOU NEED A FAMILY PHYSICIAN, please contact your local MEDICAL SOCIETY REFERRAL SERVICE, who will supply you with a list of physicians in your area.

MEDEXAM
4692 Holladay Court
Ipsilanti, Utah 84117
(801) 377-3216

Assignment 12: Correspondence Filing, #3

THOMAS P. SHERIDAN, M.D.
3306 Harbell Drive SW
Halloway, OR 97403
(503) 282-0032

August 15, 1992

To Whom It May Concern:

Re: Jacqueline Jessep
      OWCP #A14-252102

I have seen Ms. Jessep for manifestations of minor cervical joint strain with secondary cervical myofascial syndrome.

I have prescribed a Speed glass welding helmet #1. I do this because of its light weight and the fact that the latter sitting on top of the patient's head will not cause intervertebral strain that the more classic welding helmet will. I feel that when looked at over the years of further welding this woman has before her, the switch to the lightweight Speed glass could only benefit her medical-cervical status.

Your consideration in this matter is appreciated.

Sincerely,

Thomas P. Sheridan M.D.

Thomas P. Sheridan, M.D.

TPS/mlf

ASSIGNMENT #12: Correspondence Filing, #4

NATURAL THERAPEUTICS
3627 Alexandria Avenue
Portland, OR 97504
(503) 874-3342

Patient: <u>Michael D. Buskins</u>

Diagnosis: <u>Cervical myofascial syndrome</u>

MODALITIES:
HYDROTHERAPY

<u>X</u> Hot packs

___ Cold packs

MASSAGE:

<u>X</u> Medical treatment

<u>X</u> Stress reduction

___ Relaxation

___ Combination

EXERCISES:

___ Range of motion

<u>X</u> Passive

<u>X</u> Active

___ Resistive

MUSCLE STRENGTHENING:

___ Lower extremities

___ Upper extremities

TREATMENT INTERVALS: __2__ TIMES PER WEEK,

FOR __4__ WEEKS

PRECAUTIONS: _____

ANTICIPATED GOALS: <u>Reduction in muscle spasm</u>

Michael D. Stenousky RPT   *June 16, 1992*
Signature   Date

Assignment 12: Correspondence Filing, #5

THOMAS P. SHERIDAN, M.D.
3306 Harbell Drive SW
Halloway, OR 97403
(503) 282-0032

May 16, 1992

Commander
Columbia River Naval Shipyard
Astoria, OR 97103

Dear Commander:

Re: Suzette B. Murphy-Slaughter
     SS #534-02-1083

Ms. Murphy-Slaughter is a woman with multiple sclerosis. I first saw the patient in May of 1991 referred by Doctor Lasnetske for evaluation of bilateral leg numbness and slurred speech. She had given a history of numbness affecting the soles of her feet, numbness evolving up to her waist. A myelogram performed by Doctor Lasnetske was entirely normal. So too, she was experiencing 30-minute long episodes of slurred speech during which time she would have no difficulty understanding the spoken word.

The initial neurological exam revealed right upper motor neuron weakness in the right arm, the patient also having a superimposed paraparesis with 4/5 strength in the lower extremities. She had decreased vibratory sense in the lower extremities and a wide-based spastic gait. Seeing her today she does not have a cerebellar deficit but she has shown some ataxia in the upper extremities on exam. Overall she is ambulatory.

Sincerely,

Thomas P. Sheridan M.D.

Thomas P. Sheridan, M.D.

TPS/mlf

Assignment 12: Correspondence Filing, #6

THOMAS P. SHERIDAN, M.D.
3306 Harbell Drive SW
Halloway, OR 97403
(503) 282-0032

May 16, 1992

Mr. Hal Fergeson
Claims Supervisor
Sedgwick Associates
PO Box 83
Portland, OR 97207-8300

Dear Mr. Fergeson:

Re: Jack Bukins
     Claim #T-466111/90-009472

I feel that Mr. Bukins is almost medically stable. He is continuing to show benefit with Doctor Wright's efforts and I would defer to Doctor Wright in terms of his thoughts on how long chiropractic treatment will be required. There is no need for MD medical supervision in this case. As we have established, there is no threat to the neuraxis and clearly conservative measures are in order.

I have instructed the patient in all the logical do's and don't's of conservative care in the way of exercises and lifestyle modifications.

I do feel he has suffered a permanent impairment as a result of the above incident. I would feel that outside of continuation of conservative measures, including his manipulative therapy, he would be stable and ratable for closure. Again, I would defer to Doctor Wright in terms of the time requirement and I would suspect something like two more months would be a reasonable duration.

If you have any further questions, please feel free to contact me.

Sincerely,

Thomas P. Sheridan M.D.

Thomas P. Sheridan, M.D.
TPS/mlf

Assignment 12: Correspondence Filing, #7

MILLER STANTON INC.   **E. Miller Stanton**
                                                           President

PO Box 863   512-6292
Prosper, OR 98411

JOB ANALYSIS

Date: 4/30/92   LOCATION: Edna, WA

JOB TITLE: Service Center Clerk

GENERAL DESCRIPTION OF THE JOB: Customer service for grocery store customers to include public relations, sale of film, batteries, cigarettes, lotto tickets, money orders, popcorn, and miscellaneous items. Responsible for film processing, key making, UPS shipping, rental of video tapes and carpet cleaning equipment, utility bill collection and payment, and check cashing.

TYPE OF EQUIPMENT, MACHINERY OR TOOLS USED: Cash register, personal computer and printer, popcorn machine, calculator and other office equipment.

WORK HOURS: Can be 4-8   DAYS/WEEK: Can be 3-5

MEALS/BREAKS: 4 hours = one 10-minute break; 8 hours = lunch midway through shift and two 10-minute breaks during each 4-hour period.

PERCENTAGE SPENT EACH DAY:
25% Walking   10% Sitting   65% standing
            100% indoors   0% outdoors

PHYSICAL MOVEMENTS REQUIRED ON THE JOB:
C-constantly, F-frequently, O-occasionally, S-Seldom, N-never

Twisting	S	Stooping	O	Bending	O
Squatting	S	Kneeling	N	Crawling	N
Climbing:		Reaching	O	Working	
Stairs	N			at heights	N
Ladders	N				

Patient/Employee: Shirley E. Benton-Mussman

Assignment 12: Correspondence Filing, #8

THOMAS P. SHERIDAN, M.D.
3306 Harbell Drive SW
Halloway, OR 97403
(503) 282-0032

October 14, 1992

Mr. Kurt Lendelholm
Claims Adjustor
Oregon Mutual Insurance Company
10700 Meridian Avenue North
Graham, OR 97721

Dear Mr. Lendelholm:

Re: Laurel MacWilliams

I am writing in followup to you of July 8, 1992. At that time I delineated to you her history and the fact that I viewed all of the symptoms she was describing to me at that time to the effects of a June 19, 1992, accident.

At that time, based on the history and findings, I felt that the patient had sustained a cervical joint strain with secondary cervical myofascial syndrome. I felt she was describing muscle contraction headaches. I felt she had a lumbar ligamentous strain. At that time it was a bit too early for me to quote a long-term prognosis.

I next saw the patient on August 15, 1992. With the passage of time her lumbar problems were receding considerably. Her cervical pain remained. On that occasion she had limited cervical extension and right lateral rotation with mild to moderate tightness and tenderness in the cervical extensor muscles. I have not seen the patient since then.

Sincerely,

Thomas P. Sheridan, M.D.

Thomas P. Sheridan, M.D.

TPS/mlf

Assignment 12: Correspondence Filing, #9

Robert C. Andrews, M.D.
Suite 302, Bridgeview Building
Talbot, OR 97352

1853 Ohare Avenue

(503) 914-8076

Diplomate
American Board
Orthopaedic Surgery

Fellow
American Academy
of Orthopaedic Surgeons

January 24, 1992

Thomas P. Sheridan, M.D.
3306 Harbell Drive SW
Halloway, OR 97403

Dear Dr. Sheridan:

Re: Edgar S. Brown

I am referring for your reconsideration Edgar Brown, whom you evaluated at the request of Doctor Cartwright on December 15, 1991. While Edgar at that time had low-back and right lower extremity complaints, he had a myelogram showing a defect at L5-S1. He has developed objective findings of an S1 radiculopathy consisting of decreased left Achilles reflex, hypesthesia on the lateral border of his left foot and some limitation of straight-leg raising on the left. A CT scan repeated on January 6 demonstrates an L5-S1 disc herniation displacing the S1 nerve root.

I am asking that you re-evaluate him to determine if you concur with my findings.

Sincerely yours,

Roberta C. Andrews, M.D.

Roberta C. Andrews, M.D.

RCA/twp

Assignment 12: Correspondence Filing, #10

INSURANCE COMPANY OF THE WEST
1453 Ridgeway Blvd, PO Box 93025, Sunriver, OR 97707
(503) 369-2468

February 20, 1992

Thomas P. Sheridan, M.D.
3306 Harbell Drive SW
Halloway, OR 97403

RE: File #:   02-36-1447
     Insured: Newman, Heather
     Claimant: Bruce Newman
     D/Event: 6/03/90

Dear Dr. Sheridan:

We have received and thank you for your examination report dated January 3, 1992.

As this is a federal claim and not a State claim, it is necessary that you translate the rating into a percentage of loss of motion according to the AMA guidelines. Also, what part of this rating do you feel is pre-existing and what part is due to the strain of June 3, 1990.

Any expense you may incur in providing this additional information, please bill us directly. Thank you for your cooperation.

Yours very truly,

Carol Clauson

Carol Clauson
Claims Representative

CC/abw

Assignment 12: Correspondence Filing, #11

THOMAS P. SHERIDAN, M.D.
3306 Harbell Drive SW
Halloway, OR 97403
(503) 282-0032

November 19, 1992

Ms. Estelle Neuman
62408 Bettencourt Lane
Vida, OR 97408

Dear Estelle:

Re: Termination of medical care

I am writing to advise you that I will no longer be able to provide medical care for you. I would be more than happy to send a copy of your notes to whatever clinician you deem appropriate to be treating you.

You have medications that have already been prescribed, enough to last for the next month.

Sincerely,

Thomas P. Sheridan M.D.

Thomas P. Sheridan, M.D.

TPS/mlf

Assignment 12: Correspondence Filing, #12

STANDARD ADMINISTRATION INSURANCE

home office: Unionvail, Oregon 97114
PO Box 711
(503) 345- 0263

April 3, 1992

Thomas P. Sheridan, M.D.
3306 Harbell Drive SW
Halloway, OR 97403

RE: Susan St. James
     DOB: 11/13/44
     SSN: 538-26-9375
     Claim #: B8437S

Dear Dr. Sheridan:

Your patient, Susan St. James, is currently receiving long-term disability benefits from Standard Insurance Company. In order for us to better understand Ms. St. James' medical condition, please provide a report within 15 days including:
1. Description of current condition and prognosis.
2. Copies of all objective medical evidence on file.
3. Description of the treatment patient is receiving.

Enclosed is an authorization for the release of this information and a postage-paid, return envelope for your convenience. Standard is willing to pay a reasonable fee for your services. Please include a statement and your tax identification number with your reply.

Thank you for your time and assistance.

Sincerely,

Allison T. Perez
Allison T. Perez
Group Benefits Department

ATP:akj
Enclosure   **DEDICATED TO EXCELLENCE FOR POLICYOWNERS**

Assignment 12: Correspondence Filing, #13

Law Offices of
Peirson B. Johansen
43 Fourth Avenue Southeast
Portage, WA 98394
(206) 377-2963
1-800-788-0222

June 18, 1992

Thomas P. Sheridan, M.D.
3306 Harbell Drive SW
Halloway, OR 97403

Dear Dr. Sheridan:

Re: Your patient/our client: Kenneth O. King
      Date of Loss: 8/16/87

As you are aware, this office represents the above-captioned client for injuries sustained on the above-captioned date.

At this time we request that you please provide this office with a copy of your consultation report and copies of your office notes regarding our client subsequent to and including the date of loss. We are enclosing a medical release which has been executed by our client.

We would appreciate receipt of these materials by July 20, 1992, to allow us time for pre-trial review. Thank you for your prompt attention in this regard.

Sincerely,

Pierson B. Johansen

by Christopher N. Swanson
Legal Assistant

GOC/CNS:nb
Enclosure

Assignment 12: Correspondence Filing, #14

THOMAS P. SHERIDAN, M.D.
3306 Harbell Drive SW
Halloway, OR 97403
(503) 282-0032

September 3, 1992

To Whom It May Concern:

Re: Herbert B. Weinstein
        #A14-20304

Herbert Weinstein is a patient I have seen for a left carpal tunnel syndrome. The patient was injured on the job on January 10, 1985, sustaining blunt trauma to the median nerve at the wrist. Obviously with the symptoms starting immediately in association with this, we view his documented carpal tunnel syndrome as related to his industrial accident.

If you have any further questions, please feel free to contact me.

Sincerely,

Thomas P. Sheridan M.D.

Thomas P. Sheridan, M.D.

TPS/mlf

Assignment 12: Correspondence Filing, #15

THOMAS P. SHERIDAN, M.D.
3306 Harbell Drive SW
Halloway, OR 97403
(503) 282-0032

December 13, 1992

Mr. Kennison T. Thompson
Travelwell Insurance Company
PO Box 306
Portland, OR 97219

Re: Marie P. Dunnaway
      Policy #T-14093-SC

I appreciate your communicating with my office on the basis for your remuneration of $320 for my work. As you know, I did a comprehensive consult and an EMG of two extremities. I was paid $100 for the consult (diagnostic code 90260) and $110 each for the two EMGs.

I want to protest my payment for a comprehensive consult. Your payment schedule falls not only behind private insurers like Kaiser, CHAMPUS, Indemnity Hospitalization, and Lane County Employees but actually falls significantly behind Medicare, with the allowable fee for a comprehensive consult being $129 or 29% more than what you have chosen to pay. Lane County presently pays $155 for a comprehensive consult. The same applies for the EMG. Lane County reimburses presently $140 for and EMG and Kaiser $128. Indemnity considers $135 a reasonable charge. I would invite you to check to verify that what I am saying is true.

I do not know then how Travelwell can unilaterally pay so little for these same procedures. I hope that you will review your charges and arrive at a more equitable payment schedule for your policy holders.

Sincerely,

Thomas P. Sheridan M.D.

Thomas P. Sheridan, M.D.
TPS/mlf

Assignment 12: Correspondence Filing, #16

MEDRECS COPYING SERVICE, INC
Specialists in Obtaining Medical, Legal and
Employment Records

6245 Aussing Way   Seattle, WA 98195   (206) 556-8913

October 12, 1992

Thomas P. Sheridan, M.D.
3306 Harbell Drive SW
Halloway, OR 97403

RE: Kent Allen Borgetz
DOB July 12, 1955
SS #838-26-1074

Dear Dr. Sheridan:

Please find attached documents directing and authorizing you to release the records of Kent A. Borgetz.

It is VERY IMPORTANT that the attached deposition questions or declaration be filled out by the preparer of this request and RETURNED with the records by October 31, 1992.

It is important that MEDRECS obtain ONE COMPLETE COPY of ALL the following records:

EACH AND EVERY ITEM IN THE PATIENT'S CHART

Contact the undersigned if you have any questions. If it is more convenient for MEDRECS to photocopy these records at your office, please call to make arrangements.

Thank you for your cooperation:

Sincerely,

Patrick T. Taylor

Patrick T. Taylor
Customer Account Representative

PTT/joe
Enclosures

Assignment 12: Correspondence Filing, #17

PACIFIC COAST INSURANCE COMPANY

UNION BRANCH CLAIMS OFFICE
PO Box 9559
30440 Prudential Blvd. East
Union, OR 97883
(503) 473-0400
1-800-996-2239

November 7, 1992

Thomas P. Sheridan, M.D.
3306 Harbell Drive SW
Halloway, OR 97403

SUPPLEMENTAL PHYSICIAN REPORT

Date	Policyholder	Date of Loss	Pol #
11/07/92	Dwight A. Higgins	5/02/92	A140920

TO ASSIST US IN DETERMINING BENEFITS STILL DUE UNDER THE PERSONAL INJURY PROTECTION BENEFITS LAW, THE ATTENDING PHYSICIAN SHOULD COMPLETE THIS REPORT AND RETURN IT DIRECTLY

PATIENT: Erin T. Higgins

IT IS 6 MONTHS POST ACCIDENT AND TREATMENT SEEMS TO BE INCREASING:

1. Diagnosis
2. How is this patient progressing? Is treatment proceeding at expected rate?
3. When might he/she reach pre-accident status?
4. When can we expect treatment to begin decreasing?
5. If this patient is disabled, when will he/she return to previous employment?
6. Any information helpful in evaluating this claim?

Melanie Granboette   11/07/92
Signature   Date

America's Dependable Insurance Company

Assignment 12: Correspondence Filing, #18

WASHINGTON
INDUSTRIAL INSURANCE
STATE FUND

May 15, 1992

Thomas P. Sheridan, M.D.
3306 Harbell Drive SW
Halloway, OR 97403

Dear Mr. Delancey:
    Claim #M8083882

Thank you for your letter of April 6, 1992. I have asked our service location staff to reschedule this exam for you for some time after mid June. They will let you know the details.

Unfortunately, your letter did not provide a complete new address. I know your mail is being forwarded, so I am addressing this to your old address. If you are going to be in California for more than a few weeks, please provide a complete address including zip code and telephone. We cannot manage your claim unless we can communicate with you.

Regarding your exam, if your claim is to remain open, you will need to attend.

Sincerely,

Kendall B. Williams
Claims Manager
(206) 834-0322

CC

```
* * * * * * * * * * * * * * * * * * * * * * * * * * * * * * * *
*              THIS IS A COPY FOR YOUR FILES              *
* * * * * * * * * * * * * * * * * * * * * * * * * * * * * * * *
```

PROVIDER'S COPY

Patient: Victor B. Delancey

Assignment 12: Correspondence Filing, #19

THOMAS P. SHERIDAN, M.D.
3306 Harbell Drive SW
Halloway, OR 97403
(503) 282-0032

August 16, 1992

Mr. Dennis Dickinson
Claims Manager
PACIFIC COAST INSURANCE COMPANY
UNION BRANCH CLAIMS OFFICE
PO Box 9559
Union, OR 97883

Dear Mr. Dickinson:

Re: Heather Newman
      Claim #TWS-3003822

As you know, the patient was involved in an injury on June 3, 1990, being struck on her hard hat by a descending tree which sent her to the ground. The patient developed head injury symptoms of cognitive impairment together with certain visual symptoms. She was describing diplopia, visual blurring and a problem with night vision. When last seen she had 20/25 visual acuity in the right eye and 20/30 on the left with corrective lenses. Pupils were 3 mm and reactive. Funduscopic examination was unremarkable.

I have given her the name of Dr. Kim Sutherland, a neuro-ophthalmologist in Portland, as someone to consult in this matter.

Sincerely,

Thomas P. Sheridan M.D.

Thomas P. Sheridan, M.D.

TPS/mlf

Assignment 12: Correspondence Filing, #20

I. C. SYSTEM
The System Works
1103 Spinnati Way
Olympia, WA 98504-5000

September 24, 1992

Thomas P. Sheridan, M.D.
3306 Harbell Drive SW
Halloway, OR 97403

Thank you for your most recently-referred accounts. This report is being produced to confirm the debts that we have entered for you. Please note the account number that we have assigned to your debtors. By providing the assigned account number when you call or write to us, we will be able to service you better. We want to encourage you to review your accounts and refer them to I. C. System as they become 60-90 days past due. This will help to improve your accounts receivable.

As you see at the top of your report, your I. C. System collection program is now named "Premier Collect." You can continue to rely on your Premier Collect program for full service debt collection.

Sincerely,

Alex O. Mayerson

Alex O. Mayerson
Collections Manager

Enclosures

Assignment 13: Database Files

B: Birthplace
R: Where raised

#1 Alex Flores, Male, age 43; 3409 Calaspell, Gallup, NM, 87301; B: Albany, New York; R: Ithica, New York and Newark, New Jersey

#2 David Landerman, Male, age 28; 305 NE Fairground, Logan, NM, 88426; B: Cortland, New York; R: Miami, Florida, Newark, New Jersey, and Brooklyn, New York

#3 James Strader, male, age 24; 3500 Mission, Ramah, NM, 87321; B: Kalispell, Montana; R: Pocatello, Idaho

#4 Roberta Linde, female, age 22; 20201 Front NE, La Villita, NM, 87511; B: Lansing, Michigan; R: Othello, Washington and Prairie Plains, Oregon

#5 Rickey Vinson, male, age 53; 88435 Winston, Pastura, NM, 88435; B: Shelby, Washington; R: Shelby, Washington and Medford, Oregon

#6 Anthony Floreske, male, age 32; 209 Westlake, Engel, NM, 87935; B: Spokane, Washington; R: Spokane, Washington

#7 Evan Margrave, male, age 44; 6295 Prairie Lane, Jareles, NM, 87023; B: Tacoma, Washington; R: Bellingham, Washington, Federal Way, Washington, and Pittsburg, Pennsylvania

#8 William Olsen, male, age 37; 31186 Echo, Engel, NM, 87935; B: Ann Arbor, Michigan; R: Lansing, Michigan, Boise, Idaho, and Twin Falls, Idaho

#9 Jessica Kao, female, age 26; 25 Twilight, Gila, NM, 88038; B: Miami, Florida; R: Portland, Oregon and Miami, Florida

#10 Denise Romnes, female, age 22; 4928 Hilltop, Laguna, NM, 87026; B: Bellingham, WA; R: Blaine, Washington and Mesa, Arizona

#11 Janine Lutz, female, age 36; 632 Sunset, Pastura, NM, 88435; B: Houston, Texas; R: Los Angeles, California and Klamath Falls, Oregon

#12 Larry Williams, male, age 24; 633 Convex, Engel, NM, 87935; B: Los Angeles, California; R: Bakersfield, California, Portland, Oregon, and Seattle, Washington

#13 Ninette Thompson, female, age 38; 1623 Moon Rock, Crownpoint, NM, 87313; B: Lakewood, New Jersey; R: Granite Falls, New Hampshire, Richland, Washington, and Portland, Oregon

#14 Shelby Resop, female, age 27; 1111 Broadway, Rio Lucio, NM, 87553; B: Tulsa, Oklahoma; R: Hermiston, Oregon, and Oklahoma City, Oklahoma

#15 Oscar Riksheim, male, age 56; 6234 West Point, Pastura, NM, 88435; B: Boston, Massachusetts; R: Everett, Washington

#16 Kimberly Swan, female, age 22; 622 Sand Point, Rio Lucio, NM, 87553; B: Louisville, Kentucky; R: Yakima, Washington, Sweetwater, Texas, and Canyon River, Washington

#17 Cynthia Bruchaster, female, age 40; 5421 Mercer, East Pecos, NM, 87552; B: Pittsburgh, Pennsylvania; R: Pittsburgh, Pennsylvania, Port Angeles, Washington, and Forks, Washington

#18 Don Swansboro, male, age 30; 44860 Chippewa, Dexter, NM, 88230; B: Tucson, Arizona; R: Hermiston, Oregon, and Tucson, Arizona

#19 Cathe Suzuki, female, age 28; 2069 Greenway, Logan, NM, 88426; B: Salem, Oregon; R: Portland, Oregon, and Newport, Oregon

#20 David Unieski, male, age 32; 811 East 8th, Aztec, NM, 87410; B: Austin, Texas; R: Klamath Falls, Oregon, Dallas, Texas, and Salem, Oregon

#21 Sonja Yeager, female, age 28; 1861 Teppe, Navajo, NM, 87328; B: Boise, Idaho; R: Pocatello, Idaho, and Idaho Falls, Idaho

#22 Joyce Riddick, female, age 28; 3299 Macgraw, Gallup, NM, 87301; B: Paradise Valley, California; R: Spokane, Washington, and Sacramento, California

#23 Dale Holloway, male, age 36; 57631 Sunset, LaVillita, NM, 87511; B: Kimball, Virginia; R: Grangeville, Idaho, and Ketchum, Idaho

#24 Michaela Peelman, female, age 29; 7994 Commerce, Navajo, NM, 87328; B: Aberdeen, Washington; R: Westport, Washington

#25 Thomas Olanie, male, age 23; 54286 Iowa Drive, Dexter, NM, 88320; B: Pocatello, Idaho; R: Orofino, Idaho, and Kingston, North Carolina

#26 Andrew Peterson, male, age 42; 9862 West Point, Rio Lucio, NM, 87553; B: Springfield, Missouri; R: Rolla, Missouri, Scotts Butte, Oregon, and LaGrande, Oregon

#27 Vivian Shafer, female, age 34; 615 Salmon; Crownpoint, NM, 87313; B: Shawnee, Oklahoma; R: Salmona, Idaho, and Stillwater, Oklahoma

#28 Mary Alice Quilacio, female, age 22; 3296 Crescent, Jareles, NM, 87023; B: Bluefield, Virginia; R: Morgantown, Virginia, and Twin Falls, Idaho

#29 Lorraine Matson, female, age 43; 8842 Tepee Pt., Engel, NM, 87935; B: Amarillo, Texas; R: Durant, Oklahoma, Coos Bay, Oregon, and Salem, Oregon

#30 Philip Charness, male, age 27; 1600 Chester, Crownpoint, NM, 87313; B: Medford, Oregon; R: Grants Pass, Oregon, Redding, California, and Sacramento, California

APPENDIX **D**

Arrangements of Chart Materials

Strict Chronological Arrangement

With this type of filing, materials are filed strictly with the most recently charted materials at the top of the folder. For instance, a patient is followed from 1963 to 1986. If you want to locate information recorded in 1973, you would have to flip through the chart until you locate the material for the year 1973. Below is a sample of this type of patient file.

	PHYSICAL EXAMINATION 1990	CHEST X RAY 87	PHYSICAL 84	LAB WORK 81	ROBINSON, Terry L. 93 ROB

Figure D-1

Problem-Oriented Medical Record (POMR)

Internists, family practitioners, and pediatricians use this system more commonly than do specialists because they see their patients for a variety of different types of problems over a long span of time.

The main elements of this type of record keeping use a logsheet on the inside cover that lists vital identification data, immunizations, allergies, medications and problems. The problems are identified by a number that will correspond with the charting relevant to that problem number. This allows medical personnel to be aware of current medications and unresolved problems. Below is illustrated the POMR sheet as well as the charted information.

NAME _____

ADDRESS _____

INS. # _____

IMMUNIZATIONS
_____

ALLERGIES _____

MEDICATIONS _____

PROBLEM LIST:

#1 _Bronchitis 6/14/90_____

#2 _Pneumonia 6/15/89_____

#3 _Diabetes 7/04/92_____

DICTATION FOR 7/04/92

Problem #2: Pneumonia
Discussion regarding problem,
tmt., etc.

Problem #3: Diabetes
Discussion concerning status
and treatment of this condition.

Alex P. Distress, M.D.

#679-24-11941

Figure D-2

Sectioned Records

A great many offices use this method as it makes different types of information quickly accessible. Sectional records utilize a fastener-folder that contains several partitions with their own fasteners. This allows for a separate section for all lab reports, pathology, physical examinations, correspondence, etc., so that each category can be filed chronologically. See the illustration below for an example of this type of file folder.

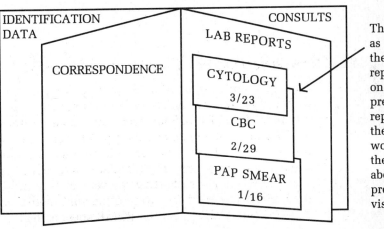

IDENTIFICATION DATA

CORRESPONDENCE

CONSULTS

LAB REPORTS

CYTOLOGY
3/23

CBC
2/29

PAP SMEAR
1/16

This is referred to as "shingling"—the most recent report is placed on top of previously–filed report, starting at the bottom and working toward the top; leaving about 1/2" of previous report visible.

Chart Labeling

There is no absolute standard for what a chart label must contain. You will find that most offices custom-make their labels to suit their needs. Following are some of the most common types of labeling methods, each tailored to provide information the individual office feels is most relevant. Regardless of content, the labels are located on the tab that is visible when the chart is being retrieved. For some that is the tab running from top to bottom on the long side of the chart:

JAMES, Howard T.   89   DOB 4/17/47

and for others it is the tab running from side to side on the narrower side of the chart:

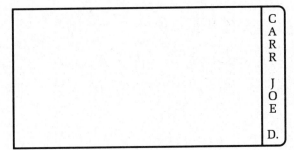

789 29 5539

Color-coded #, filed by terminal digit.

LAST NAME, First Middle

Color-coded folder, white label; red dots are used to alert personnel to identical names so they know to look at DOB and address to ensure correct chart.

LAST NAME, First Middle Phone #

Color-coded folder.

LAST NAME, First Middle Social Security # DOB	Acct # Insurance Company Name Insurance #

LAST NAME, First Middle 93[1] Referring Doctor DOB	C[2]	CC[3]

[1]—Color-coded year sticker
[2]—Color-coded sticker, first letter of doctor's last name.
[3]—Color-coded stickers, first two letters of patient's last name.

LAST NAME, First Middle	ID #89 90 50 221

Using terminal digit filing.

Facility Name and Address[1] Return on policy[2] LAST NAME, First Middle Location of other records[4]	Patient #322 89 99988 240[3]

[1]—Preprinted on label; used by facility with several facilities.
[2]—Preprinted on label to indicate, for example, six-month checkup, post-surgery, etc.
[3]—Satellite, microfiche, volume #, surgery center, etc.
[4]—Chart filed by terminal digit number.

```
┌─────────────────────────────────────┐
│ LAST NAME, First Middle              │     Terminal Digit Filing
│ Medical #        DOB                 │
└─────────────────────────────────────┘
```

```
┌───────────────────────────────────────────────────────────────┐
│ Date of Service                              DOB                │
│ LAST NAME, First Middle                                        │
│ Referring Physician                          Type of Exam Performed │
│ Brief Clinical History                                         │
└───────────────────────────────────────────────────────────────┘
```

This label is used by a radiology clinic. They type a large label on both the front of the original X-ray jacket and an identical card in a card file.

```
┌───────────────────────────────────────────────────────────────┐
│ LAST NAME, First Middle                                        │
│ DOB                          [1]                    XYZ         │
└───────────────────────────────────────────────────────────────┘
```

[1]—White label.
[2]—Alpha-Z labels.

```
┌───────────────────────────────────────────────────────────────┐
│ LAST NAME, First Middle[1]                                     │
│ Address                                             XYZ[2]      │
│ Phone #                                                        │
│ Guarantor's name                                               │
│ DOB                                                            │
└───────────────────────────────────────────────────────────────┘
```

[1]—White label.
[2]—Alphz-Z label; an identical label is placed on each document filed in the chart.

Index